Dear Antoine
or
The Love That Failed

Jean Anouilh's new play, *Dear Antoine*, which was first presented at the 1971 Chichester Festival, shows a group of people summoned to a remote baroque mansion in the Bavarian mountains to hear the reading of the will of a successful playwright, Antoine de Saint Flour. The season is winter, the year 1913. The men and women who have come together so reluctantly include the playwright's wife, a few friends and several ex-mistresses from different periods of his life. In confronting one another they are uneasily aware that they are confronting different reflections of Antoine's own fascinating and maddening personality. This poignantly introspective but fiercely witty play displays to the full Anouilh's masterly command of theatrical sleight of hand.

'A dazzling *tour de force*.' Harold Hobson in the *Sunday Times*.

The photograph on the front cover shows Dame Edith Evans and Sir John Clements in a scene from the Chichester production and is reproduced by courtesy of John Timberr. The photograph on the back of the cover is reproduced by courtesy of Jane Bown.

D0921281

Jean Anouilh

DEAR ANTOINE
or
The Love That Failed

Translated by
LUCIENNE HILL

METHUEN & CO LTD
11 NEW FETTER LANE LONDON EC4

First published in Great Britain by
Methuen & Co Ltd in 1971.
Copyright © 1971 by Jean Anouilh and Lucienne Hill
Printed in Great Britain by
Cox & Wyman Ltd, Fakenham, Norfolk

SBN 416 66870 4 Hardback
SBN 416 66880 1 Paperback

Dear Antoine was first presented at the Chichester Festival Theatre on 19 May 1971 with the following cast:

MARCELLIN	Hubert Gregg
ESTELLE	Joyce Redman
VALÉRIE	Renée Asherson
ANÉMONE	Polly Adams
CARLOTTA	Edith Evans
CRAVATAR	Michael Aldridge
LAPINET	Clive Swift
LAWYER	Harold Innocent
GABRIELLE	Jane Baxter
ALEXANDER	Peter Egan
MARIA	Joanna David
FRIDA	Peggy Marshall
ALEXIS	James Faulkner
ANTOINE	John Clements
SERVING LAD	Paul Hastings

Directed by Robin Phillips

*

The action takes place in Bavaria in 1913

Act One

The main hall of a big old mansion, foreign baroque in style. Enter, in travelling clothes, a young woman in mourning, and a man, also in black. They appear to be looking over the house for the first time.

MARCELLIN. A little gem of baroque decoration in a sixteenth-century setting. It's splendid.

ESTELLE (*detached*). Yes, Antoine always did have splendid houses. It was a disease with him. Whenever he liked a place, he had to buy a house there. As he grew older, so it grew worse. In the end he began to think that buying a new house was the solution to every difficulty. Our separation, or rather – his estrangement – he never asked me to divorce him – was strewn with Heaven knows how many property acquisitions. He'd convinced himself – just because we'd spent the happiest part of our honeymoon there – that Florence should be the scene of our reconciliation. Any other man would have taken a suite at the Grand Hotel, he bought a villa at Fiesole, where we only spent one day. Just time for a quarrel – a final one as it turned out. Later on, when we decided – mutually – to send Philippe away to school, the very thought of seeing the boy on Sundays in a restaurant made him quite ill. So he bought a house two miles away. Four walls and a roof were his way of believing in the family. He never asked himself what was to be put inside. I must say it was a very pretty house – a Norman manor. Taste, in Antoine, was the one thing you could totally rely on. We had lunch there on four separate Sundays – as a family – that is, without saying a single word, surrounded by devoted servants who are still there waiting I should think. Another small point – he had the unfailing secret, wherever he went, of engaging domestic staff who all adored him. (*She shrugs bitterly.*) If you can call it a secret. The young maids got caresses

– the old ones were treated like queens and given a kiss on the cheek.

MARCELLIN. Theatrical custom! Antoine always kissed everybody.

ESTELLE (*without reacting*). When I eventually took Philippe away from boarding school and back to Paris with me, Antoine was already living here, in Bavaria, with that girl. And for her, of course, he could hardly do less than buy a castle. Faced with the problem of his monthly visit to the children (he refused to come back home to the Avenue Foch – although I was more than glad to receive him) you'd think he'd have taken a room at the Ritz. Not Antoine. For this new piece of family adultery, he bought and furnished a bachelor flat in Montmartre, where the concierge, who knew the local morals, made I don't know how many reports to the police to say that her new tenant was corrupting boys and girls of tender age – Marie-Christine and Philippe went there, you see, by turns, to spend the night. Grandchâtre, the Préfêt, even sent for him, very concerned, and urged him to be a little more discreet in his vices.

MARCELLIN. How wildly funny!

ESTELLE. Wasn't it? I schooled myself, with Antoine, always to treat everything as wildly funny. I spent fifteen years flaunting screams of laughter and floods of tears.

MARCELLIN. Poor Estelle!

ESTELLE (*echoing him*). Poor Estelle. That's what everyone in Paris said. I used to be just Estelle. I won myself a second name. Poor-Estelle with a hyphen. Poor! Winning little name. One that suits me so well. Don't you think so?

MARCELLIN (*nearing her*). You're maligning yourself. There are lots of men I know – myself included, I may say – who —

ESTELLE (*interrupting*). Spare me that old song. I'd decided in our lopsided relationship that one of us at least would remain faithful – to balance things a little.

MARCELLIN. Faithful to whom? To what?

ESTELLE (*briefly*). To myself, let's say. (*She looks round and exclaims.*) You must admit he lodged her fairly well, that last little thing.

MARCELLIN. Did you never come here?

ESTELLE. Never, of course not. Antoine's policy with his various houses was based on total isolation. So then, after several unsuccessful love affairs – which made him the owner of a small house at Versailles, a mansion in Brittany and a villa in Cannes – and what was rather more original – a houseboat on the Loire – he finally settled for this girl (twenty-five years younger than himself) and suddenly found he needed the altitude of the Bavarian Alps. This last love of his could only breathe at four thousand feet. No one ever knew quite why. When this young creature left him last year, his mainspring must have grown a little slack, I think. He didn't see fit to acquire any other residence, for the rest of the time he was to spend alone. The lawyer did tell me though, that he'd had something else built for himself. A very fine baroque chapel, not a usual sight in this farm labourers' cemetery.

MARCELLIN. Poor Estelle!

ESTELLE (*lightly and dryly*). Poor Estelle. I shed my last tears when I heard of his miserable death. But I was so overdrawn on my weeping capital – my eyes are dry now. For life.

MARCELLIN (*in a murmur*). Cleaning his twelve bore . . .

ESTELLE (*far away*). All alone, at five in the morning, in the rising sun. He knew about guns, he'd collected them since he was a boy, he had even more of them than he had houses, and he'd been a crack shot all his life . . .

MARCELLIN (*gravely, in so far as his incurable optimism will allow*). Estelle, I was his doctor and his friend – and I told you, I've never questioned the verdict of accidental death. The only thing that grieved me – well, I mean to say, of course his dying grieved me – the only thing that shocked me, was the strict orders he left his lawyer not to let any of us know. To bury him first and only after that to telegraph to Paris.

ESTELLE (*non-committally*). Yes. He chose the little bier on wheels the poor have, it seems, pulled by hand, the way they do in these parts. Even the servants had orders not to follow him. He left alone, for his lovely baroque chapel. His last house. (*She adds crisply.*) That one we'll keep. But we'll have to sell the others. When and how though? Marie-Christine and Philippe are still under age.

A pause.

MARCELLIN (*with emotion as he points to a table*). His desk. That's where he must have sat writing.

ESTELLE (*dryly*). He hadn't written a line since he left me.

MARCELLIN (*after another pause*). Do you think he was in love with that girl?

ESTELLE (*distinctly*). I always forbade myself that question. I've a taste for simplification.

Enter VALÉRIE, *a young woman of* ESTELLE'S *age, in a sort of half-mourning, but most discreet, followed by her very young daughter*, ANÉMONE.

VALÉRIE. What an extraordinary house! And it looks just like him too. I wonder how he managed, always, in so many different climates, to find something in his own image.

ESTELLE (*dryly*). If he'd fallen in love with an Eskimo, I'm sure he'd have managed to set his personal stamp on an igloo. But I never went to view any of the others, it must be something lacking in my nature. You've an advantage over me, Valérie, you did come to my house. Antoine did his entertaining in his wife's home. Tell me, that little hunting lodge in Sologne that he bought in your day, was that in his own image too?

VALÉRIE (*distinctly*). My dear Estelle, do remember that we agreed, when we made it up, never to mention any of that again?

ESTELLE. Yes, we did. I'm sorry, Valérie. But I'm sure you can see how coming to his last haven might make me regret not having seen yours. (*She adds without a break, charmingly.*) That discreet half-mourning suits you wonderfully. You really do have infinite tact, Valérie! Some would have come as sham widows (in fact your amours were eternal – two years!) You've always known how to behave beautifully in any circumstances. Even Anémone, by some subtle interplay of mother-daughter dress sense, has contrived a whiff of mourning – no more – in the touches of black on that little grey suit. I recognize the invaluable guidance of her mamma.

ANÉMONE (*with surprising aggressiveness*). My dear Estelle, I cared very deeply for Antoine. His death gave me great pain and I needed no guiding hand to stop me turning up in shocking pink. I might add that I find yours and mamma's little rearguard skirmishings quite exasperating. If the lawyer hadn't stressed Antoine's urgent request that I should be present at the reading of his will, I shouldn't have come. And certainly not in cavalcade.

ESTELLE (*bitterly*). My dear Valérie – this I can say, it's outside our agreement – I think your daughter is terribly badly brought up.

VALÉRIE (*smoothly*). Our children are all very badly brought up, Estelle. But I might point out that child-rearing is a skill to which we've never devoted much attention.

MARCELLIN (*prudently*). Anyway we haven't come here to squabble. We've come in answer to Antoine's sacred wish that we should all be present in his last house when his will is read. What can the others be doing?

ESTELLE. There's only one, very narrow, road up to here, and only one available motor vehicle with chains that can comfortably climb to this level in snow. The driver has undertaken to ferry our whole party. In three trips everybody will be here.

MARCELLIN. In all the crush in the station buffet at Munich this morning, I couldn't see who was there and who wasn't. I caught a glimpse of Cravatar. Will Carlotta be coming?

ESTELLE (*acidly*). Of course! The great man's first wife!

MARCELLIN. Don't be acrimonious, Estelle, that's ancient history.

ESTELLE. It's archaeology! Carlotta's a historical monument now.

MARCELLIN (*heartfelt*). Believe it or not, she's still tremendous. I saw her Phèdre a fortnight ago, at the gala performance for the King of Bulgaria. It was a triumph.

ESTELLE. Carlotta deals in triumphs – she has done since the end of the century. After each of the rare performances she graciously deigns to bestow on us, the students always unharness her carriage. The trouble is, they're getting old as well. She ought to get her publicity man to change them. They don't look quite like students any more.

MARCELLIN (*laughing*). How malicious you are, Estelle.

ESTELLE. What would be left to Poor-Estelle if she wasn't entitled to a little malice? A deserted wife has to find some little thing to fill her time. Some devote themselves to charity or needlepoint, I took to bitchery.

VALÉRIE. Estelle, my love, luckily I know you're acting a part just now. You're grieving, that's all, as we all are. More than we are, I expect. It was to you that Antoine gave his name.

ESTELLE (*in a different tone of voice, strange, a little muffled*). Yes, it is grief. But I've had that for so long, over so many things, that I get it mixed up a little sometimes. I'm not quite sure any more who it is I resent, and for what. Everybody, I suppose – for everything.

From outside in the courtyard, comes the sound of a motor stopping with a few disquieting bangs.

MARCELLIN. Ah! There's the second contingent intact. I don't mind telling you I shook with fright all the way up here. To begin with, there were a shade too many precipices for my liking. And then I kept feeling that that self-propelled contraption was going to explode before we got to the top. Do you believe in all this mechanical traction? I saw a gorgeous sleigh in the stables with gilded Gorgons' heads on the front. I'd have liked a ride in *that* . . .

ESTELLE. The lawyer told me it was one of Ludwig II of Bavaria's sleighs, that Antoine managed to acquire at an impossible price. But there aren't any horses to harness it with. He ordered them to be sold two days before he died. He was very fond of his horses. That was the Sultan in him. If he'd been allowed to immolate his widows too, you can be sure he'd have done it.

Enter CARLOTTA, *swathed in dark veils and topped with paradise plumes like a Shakespearean queen;* CRAVATAR, *a youngish-looking man still, a little desiccated; and* LAPINET, *a pontificating university don. Later the* LAWYER *will appear; a fat, inscrutable frockcoated German. All the men, despite their top coats, mufflers and fur gloves, are incongruously wearing top hats.*

CARLOTTA. Admirable road! Fabulous precipices! Delicious sensation of danger! House and setting both extraordinary! All of it perfection! (*She kisses* VALÉRIE *theatrically.*) Another kiss, cara mia.

ESTELLE (*sotto voce to* MARCELLIN). She always sounds like a telegram.

CARLOTTA (*pretending to discover her mistake*). Oh what a dizzy silly I am! Both of them in black, both so sad, I thought it was Estelle! I'm so sorry, dear girl. (*She goes to* ESTELLE.) It was you I meant to kiss, cara mia! (*She clasps her vigorously to her vast bosom.*) Without resentment and with all my heart. Oh, the immense, immense grief of it! I knew him so young. He looked like an amorous little telegraph boy haunting the wings of the Comédie Française.

ESTELLE (*immediately truculent*). Why a telegraph boy?

CARLOTTA (*with a burst of sudden laughter*). Because he always wore blue, dear girl! And because he sent me a telegram every morning. Every day, at dawn, round about noon, with my breakfast coffee, a rose and telegram, so long that the post office had to join a bit on to the form. Endearing, don't you think? (*She breaks into her famous laugh and then stops suddenly, tragic.*) It's abominable, all of it. Abominable. This bottomless, bottomless sorrow. Let us sit down. (*She sits in a big gilt armchair.*) Beautiful stage chair. He always did have a gift for unearthing a piece nobody had ever seen before. The unbending grandeur of the seventeenth century with a rather Germanic excess of gilt. (*She rises suddenly.*) Unsittable on. I'll try the sofa. Who are we waiting for?

> *Everyone has turned to the* LAWYER *who has been standing there stiffly for a minute or two.*

LAWYER (*he has no accent, but his phrasing has odd breaks in it*). I have sent the motor back once more to the station. (*He pulls a list out of his pocket.*) Before I can proceed to the reading of the will, I require the presence of Madame Duchemin and her son Alexander and Frau Staufenbach, *née* Werner.

ESTELLE (*with a cry*). Maria Werner?

LAWYER (*impassively*). Quite so. Frau Maria Staufenbach, *née* Werner. That is the last name on my list.

ESTELLE. And that girl agreed to come?

LAWYER. I had great difficulty finding her address. She lives in Würzburg now. I informed her of Monsieur de St Flour's express request and she agreed to come.

ESTELLE (*stiffening*). I cannot be present at the same time as that creature. You'll have to choose between her and me, sir.

LAWYER. That, dear lady, is quite impossible. I have strict instructions, and I cannot open the will until all beneficiaries are present or represented by an official proxy bearing the necessary authority.

ESTELLE. Oh, but really! Do you know who this Maria Werner was?

CARLOTTA (*going to her*). Estelle! Cara mia! Despite your immense, immense sorrow, you mustn't think like a little suburban housewife. Antoine was an exceptional man and we owe him an exceptional standard of behaviour. *Valérie's* here, isn't she?

ESTELLE (*piqued*). Valérie is my friend.

CARLOTTA. And *I'm* here! *I* had to swallow the pain and the affront of it when Antoine asked you to marry him. And *we* were an indissoluble couple!

ESTELLE. You were unfaithful to him for ten years with everyone in town – and so was he!

CARLOTTA (*peremptorily*). That's why we were indissoluble. How pretty it is, suddenly, when it gets cross ... Just like a little girl, still! You should get cross more often, cara mia, it lends you character. When Antoine lost his head over you, I understood perfectly well his wanting a young girl of good family and the smooth waters of marriage and the cries of children all around. It was one great party to him, he'd never seen any. It's so very human. I forced down my grief and let him go. And yet I was broken. The night of the wedding, I was due to appear as Andromache. I merely asked the stage manager for a stick to lean on and I played it! I sobbed from the first line to the last and that Crucifixion became a triumph. The whole of Paris knew, of course, and had come to see the death of the bull. Next morning I was cured, cured under a mountain of flowers. Yes, dear girl, I had more bouquets than you did, that day! Give! Give! Let that young person come, since he so expressly wanted her to be here. I must say, I'm most curious to know what sort of creature she can be. I was told she was a perfect fright.

VALÉRIE (*with a smile*). That would surprise me, in Antoine. Lacking all other depth of feeling, he was maniacally obsessed with beauty.

CARLOTTA (*who has sunk back on to her sofa, says confidentially to her neighbour,* CRAVATAR). I am all in, dear boy. I'm like Sarah, I never could bear heights. That's about all she and I have in common, the old monster.

MARCELLIN (*suddenly, after a pause*). This Madame Duchemin who's been sent for too ... Who's she, I wonder? I never heard of any Madame Duchemin. Does the name mean anything to you, Estelle?

ESTELLE (*bitterly*). My address books were too small to include the names of all of Antoine's mistresses. I should have needed the directory!

MARCELLIN. If Antoine summoned her here today, she must have played an important part in his life. Does it mean anything to you, Valérie?

VALÉRIE. No.

MARCELLIN (*to the* LAWYER). Have you seen this person?

LAWYER. I have merely corresponded with her. And although bound by professional secrecy, I think I can tell you – as I asked you all for your birth certificates as proof of identification – that she is a person somewhat advanced in years.

MARCELLIN. The plot thickens! How old, tell us, so we can place her?

LAWYER. Our German professional secrecy is not quite so flexible as yours, Monsieur. A person somewhat advanced in years. That is all I can tell you.

MARCELLIN. A friend of his youth – Lapinet, rack that schoolmaster's mind of yours. Have you any ideas?

LAPINET (*after a pause*). Would this person's christian name be Gabrielle?

LAWYER (*leafing through his list*). Gabrielle. That is correct. I think I can safely tell you that.

They all turn to LAPINET, *who is standing there, as if stunned.*

MARCELLIN. Well, Lapinet. Is she from your student days, this Madame Duchemin?

LAPINET (*with a faint smile, as if moved by a distant memory*). Friendship has its professional secrets too. All I can tell you is that we did know, both of us, a girl in the Latin Quarter, who was called Gabrielle Blancmesnil.

He turns, despite himself, to a big antique mirror near by and studies himself dejectedly. Instinctively his hand moves to his

bald head. He goes back to the sofa and flops down beside
CARLOTTA, *murmuring.*

Gabrielle Blancmesnil! My God, how far back it all is!

CARLOTTA. You look quite cast down suddenly, dear man.

LAPINET. Yes. It's the ghost of that girl coming in unexpectedly like this. Time passes, dear friend, time flies.

CARLOTTA (*sombrely, rigid as an idol*). No. Time doesn't exist.

LAPINET. Maybe not. But mirrors do.

CARLOTTA (*granite-like, mysterious*). You must turn your mirrors to the wall. They're traps for the spineless. I never look at myself except in one of my old portraits. I have some splendid ones by the greatest painters of our time. They're all I need.

ESTELLE (*smoothly*). Perhaps that's why you always wear a little too much rouge, Carlotta.

CARLOTTA (*steely*). Quite so, my dear, I paint my face. My model is Carlotta. And every morning, I paint the portrait of Carlotta, the one her admirers imagine her to be. It's out of the question for me to turn myself out as a demure little lady like yourself. Nobody would recognize me.

MARCELLIN (*lifting a hand to quell* ESTELLE'S *retort*). No scenes! No scenes! We are all gathered here together in loving memory of Antoine.

A pause.

VALÉRIE (*with a smile*). You'd think we were doing one of his plays. He adored this kind of theatrical situation.

CRAVATAR (*tersely*). And did he pile it on! *Not* the best aspect of his dramatic works.

CARLOTTA. Tremendous dramas! Tremendous! Imperishable! Great, great theatre!

CRAVATAR (*guardedly, ringing a little untrue*). Great theatre, yes, of its period. But since the great intellectual breakthrough, the surge of youth . . . There is a muscularity, a rush of new blood

B

... Look at Bataille, look at young Bernstein! It's all on the move!

CARLOTTA (*cutting in stiffly*). Youth – I don't know what people mean by youth. It's a very shortlived complaint. I have my public. He had his public too, right to the end. A huge public. Huge theatre. Let us bow before it.

CRAVATAR (*nettled*). As you wish. (*He leans over to* LAPINET.) Do you think he believed in it?

LAPINET. In what?

CRAVATAR. His sort of theatre.

LAPINET (*after some slight hesitation*). There's a lot to be said on that score. He was a very cultured man. Did you ever read his early poems?

CRAVATAR. Years ago.

LAPINET (*quite without malice*). Read them again. They're the best thing he ever wrote.

CRAVATAR. But then, all that success —

LAPINET (*cautiously*). It's a slippery slope. And then again, with all those houses of his, he was terribly in need of the royalties. Very expensive, my dear fellow – disorderly living.

A pause. A dog is heard howling outside.

MARCELLIN (*anxiously, going over to the* LAWYER). What's that?

LAWYER. His dog. It howls day and night since its master died.

MARCELLIN *has gone over to one of the tall windows. He murmurs.*

MARCELLIN. The snow's falling twice as thick now.

LAWYER. Yes. I think we are in for some very bad weather. Most regrettable, in view of the visit to the cemetery. Monsieur de St Flour wanted us to foregather in his chapel, after the reading of the will. That request is, of course, sacred and I think everyone here would want to comply. But the little graveyard is high up on the mountain-side and there is no way of reaching it except on foot – along a path which is feet deep in snow today.

CARLOTTA (*exclaiming*). That will be jolly!

ESTELLE (*acidly*). I hardly think, Carlotta, that, even in fine weather, jolly would be quite the word for it.

CARLOTTA (*sombrely*). Stop playing games, Estelle. You know perfectly well it's a manner of speaking. Grief is one thing and rheumatism is another. When you're my age – and you will be – you'll know that it can sometimes be an act of heroism to stay on your feet.

MARCELLIN (*going to her and kissing her hand, alarmed by her tirade*). Dearest friend – dearest friend – keep calm. We're all here to honour Antoine's memory.

The LAWYER, *his back to the others, is watching the snow. He murmurs after a pause.*

LAWYER. Our German rawness . . . Monsieur de St Flour, who was a Western European, learnt to love our German rawness. He loved bad weather. Some winters he was snowed up here for several weeks without complaining.

ESTELLE (*with a dry little laugh*). Antoine? Who was always complaining about everything? You amaze me. He was a man who valued nothing but ease and comfort. Unless they changed him for us.

MARCELLIN (*a little anxiously to the* LAWYER, *after a pause*). Can one really get snowed up here?

LAWYER. At this time of year, very seldom. Although winter was very early this year. But the position of this house, which is exceptional incidentally, does have a serious drawback at certain times. The road down to the town is a corridor of avalanches.

MARCELLIN (*elaborately casual*). And they fall, do they, those – things?

LAWYER (*with a smile*). Sometimes. The problem is to get past first. There's no danger here. It's the highest spot for miles around.

MARCELLIN. And . . . if they do fall, while one's here, what does one do?

LAWYER. One waits until they clear the road, dear sir.

MARCELLIN. Does that take long?

LAWYER. We have rather meagre means at our disposal, man-power, shovels. All the village men get down to it. Two days – three, it depends on the size of the fall. That's mountain life!

MARCELLIN. I understand. But in a case of urgency, visitors from Paris like ourselves . . . I know there's nothing to fear at this time of year, but still, I have a very important session at the Academy of Medicine on Friday . . .

LAWYER (*with a little smile*). In this remote corner of Bavaria nobody made any provision for visitors from Paris. I very much fear they may not be released any quicker than anybody else.

Another short pause.

VALÉRIE (*softly, with a smile*). I hope you notice that this is getting more and more like one of Antoine's plays. People come here, there and everywhere, on some chance pretext, with no desire to meet, yet flung together by some outside agency, somewhere. It's a very old theatrical device and he adored it. He used it again and again.

CRAVATAR (*dryly*). At least three times. *The Castle in Denmark, Bluebeard Wives,* and *The Snare.* (*He adds.*) Not, incidentally, his best plays.

LAPINET (*going to him*). Why was he so fond of tricks though? Was it a lack of strength? His dialogue was excellent, clean, crisp, quite uncluttered. He wasn't incapable of insight into emotional truths, far from it. His *Andromache* is on the syllabus of several universities in Germany and across the Atlantic.

CRAVATAR (*grudgingly*). His *Andromache* yes, I agree. Even then —

LAPINET. He was bred on the classic and he valued nothing so highly as starkness, unity, style. So why these constant theatrical pyrotechnics?

VALÉRIE (*gently*). I haven't studied his work very much. I don't think I've seen all of his plays, even. He wrote so many. But he often used to say that it amused him. And he was entitled to have fun out of it himself. That was the aristocrat in him, he loathed earnestness and effort – in everything.

LAPINET (*very much the academic*). To think what he might have achieved, gifted as he was, with a little application! Genius is an infinite capacity, etc. . . . But no! This facile, everlasting careless-ness —

VALÉRIE (*gently*). Or contempt. He used to say that literature, whatever anyone may think, was no more than the diversion of a moment. He said that Racine thought so too.

LAPINET (*with an irritated shrug*). Paradox.

CRAVATAR (*sourly*). I'm afraid his pseudo-seigneurial contempt for literature (after all, he came from a well-born legal family, no more) led him at times into some pretty poor writing.

VALÉRIE. I don't know. I'm not drama critic of the *Gaulois* like you, Cravatar. Anyway, I know he never bothered his head about that.

CRAVATAR (*sourly*). Perhaps he should have. You scoff at litera-ture, it's the done thing, you despise it – and then literature takes its revenge.

ESTELLE (*a little nettled*). I see he told you a lot of things, Valérie. They were tutorials, those afternoon interludes of yours.

VALÉRIE (*smoothly*). Not exclusively, Estelle.

A pause like the whirr of invisible wings. The dog howls outside.
CRAVATAR *swings round, growling.*

CRAVATAR. It's getting on my nerves, that dog!

LAWYER. Yes. Nobody has yet managed to quieten the poor creature down. The village people say it will have to be destroyed.

VALÉRIE. Antoine's dog? Oh no! How horrible!

A pause.

ESTELLE (*coolly*). When the house is sold, they'll find a home for it, that's all.

A pause. CARLOTTA, *who had dozed off rigidly on her stick gives a start, woken suddenly by the dog's renewed howling.*

CARLOTTA (*with a cry*). What's happening? Where have we got to? Was that my entrance?

MARCELLIN (*rushing to her*). Carlotta – dear dear friend . . . take a hold of yourself . . .

CARLOTTA (*wildly*). Where am I?

MARCELLIN (*talking as if to a child*). In Antoine's house. Our dear Antoine . . . In Bavaria – in his beautiful castle, for the reading of his will.

CARLOTTA (*coming back to earth*). Oh, good then. I thought I'd missed my cue. That stage manager's an ass, he always wakes me up too late. Yes, that's right. Antoine's dead. Is it still snowing?

MARCELLIN (*lugubriously*). Yes.

CARLOTTA (*darkly*). I can feel it in my left leg. Is there any aspirin in this place?

MARCELLIN (*to the* LAWYER). Is there any aspirin?

LAWYER. I shall move Heaven and Earth to find you some, Madame.

He ceremoniously clicks his heels and goes out.

CARLOTTA (*heavily*). Germany gives me the creeps. So do the Germans. They rob you of Alsace and Lorraine and then they click their heels at you and get you aspirin. And for a start, you get twinges in your knee in their damn country! Snow, I'll give them snow. God rot them! In Paris they fling salt on it, simple! Savages! Teutonic swine! What do you think of Goethe – like him? Werther bores me to death, always did. Wagner I can forgive them for. He deals in guts and tripe, and tripe is all I believe in. It's what I sell myself, only with them it drags on all night. And I'll tell you something else; Bayreuth is one colossal bore. And the food's awful! Don't know how to live, those folk, never have! (*She struggles painfully to her feet, leaning on her stick.*) I've got to walk about or I'll get stiff as a board.

She starts to walk up and down with her stick in the darkening room. As the light grows more and more dim, she disappears in the dark areas of the vast hall and reappears from time to time, like a Shakespearean ghost, during the ensuing scene. The young women have moved away as well.

CRAVATAR (*going to* LAPINET *who is watching the falling snow-flakes*). Odd, this idea of ending his life in Germany. So foreign to him, basically, Germany.

LAPINET. He had a German nursemaid, as a child, he often spoke of her. And I don't think he got anything much from his mother but hasty kisses on the brow at bedtime, before opera balls, in paradise plumes and spangled satin. The Viscountess de St Flour was a great lady of fashion at the turn of the century. And he grew, as a result, very attached to that other woman, as a child. He was always referring to the shock he had at eight years old, when they decided to send him away to school with the Jesuits. Childhood impressions had a very great bearing on his life.

He adds in a lower tone with a glance at ESTELLE, *who is inspecting the gallery upstage, with* VALÉRIE.

Besides he had a taste for German women – I believe that last girl of his was German too. In a world where the women of New York and Paris ruled supreme he said they were the last real women left . . .

CRAVATAR (*cackling*). Gentle Gretchen! He was a fearful romantic basically. The bluebird of happiness. His plays reek of sentiment. I dare say that's what drove him to adapt that absurd thing of Kleist's *Das Kätchen Von Heilbronn* – dismal failure it was too.

LAPINET (*pursuing his own train of thought*). And then again, that irresistible urge towards buffoonery – worse, towards ribaldry and cynicism. I must confess I've blushed like an old maid at some of his plays. You'd almost have thought him sexually obsessed, and yet —

CRAVATAR (*cutting in*). Infantilism, dear fellow. The pretty blue-bird and the little potty spillings and nothing in between. It's a stage men grow out of, he didn't, that's all. Infantilism! It's like his politics – two centuries out of date! Fundamentally, there was something retarded about him.

LAPINET (*quietly*). You're quick to judge. I know you're the most trenchant critic in town – it's what made you the pundit you are – but men are strange animals, Cravatar, and they won't be turned into a formula as easily as authors. Under his surface levity, Antoine was a fairly enigmatic man.

CRAVATAR. There's nothing so enigmatic as people with nothing much to say.

The dog has started to howl again in the courtyard outside.

CRAVATAR (*striding irritably away from the window*). I don't know about you, but that dog's driving me mad.

MARCELLIN (*who has joined them says darkly*). My dear fellows, I think we ought to lay down some pattern of conduct, don't you? We're men, we cared about Antoine and we've got to do our utmost to see that this confrontation doesn't degenerate into a brawl. This Madame Duchemin seems harmless enough – Antoine's love life at twenty, I ask you – there must be *some* time limit! But the thought of Estelle, in her present nervous state, coming face to face with her husband's last mistress sends a chill right through me. I know Antoine was a fiendish joker but he could have spared us that! What do you suggest we do?

LAPINET. We'll have to talk to Estelle.

MARCELLIN. Quite so, my dear Lapinet, but what are we to say to her?

CRAVATAR (*suddenly*). Shall I tell you what I think? Antoine was an out and out swine and that's about it. God dammit all! Deceive your wife, fine! – But be discreet about it. And if you give up the ghost and you want to provide for your little lady friend you make her an unobtrusive legacy, under an alias if need be. You don't summon her – along with your wife – to the reading of your will! (*He paces about, fuming.*) And for a start, you get a lawyer in Paris! You don't ship your entire personnel out to Bavaria, at 5,000 feet above sea level, in the very middle of winter! That's theatre. Very bad theatre at that. May I be frank? He just decided to indulge himself and thumb his nose at us, as usual, did your beloved Antoine.

He has shouted this with such venom that MARCELLIN *asks quietly.*

MARCELLIN. But then, why did you come, Cravatar?

CRAVATAR (*after a second's hesitation*). I'm not in the will. The paper sent me.

MARCELLIN (*maliciously*). Do you do the social chitchat now, Cravatar?

CRAVATAR (*vexed*). Obviously not. But Meyer was very fond of Antoine. I can't think what they could ever have been up to, the pair of them. He's devoting half an issue to a panegyric on Antoine and he wants it as spectacular as possible. Don't worry, I'll do a very good piece in the spirit required by the board of editors.

A short pause.

LAPINET (*a little pained*). Antoine thought very highly of you, Cravatar, in spite of your bad reviews. He said you were vital to the well-being of the French theatre. Being utterly devoid of it himself, he had a passion for sound sense! He used to say it was like soup, you had to swallow it down, like it or not.

CRAVATAR (*shrugging, offended*). Like soup . . . Very profound philosophical views for a writer of pot-boilers and bad melodrama.

LAPINET (*quietly*). You're wrong to shrug it off, Cravatar. His play-writing was a thing he treated rather casually, true – but

Antoine was very intelligent – enough to admit it, as he used to say with a laugh – at any rate quite as much as the experts in the field. Only he didn't like making use of his intelligence. He said it was onanism.

CRAVATAR (*hissing*). Perhaps such abstention was quite simply caution?

The dog has started howling again. CRAVATAR *seizes a stick from somewhere and goes out shouting and fuming.*

Right! I'm stopping that dog's noise! (*He goes out.*)

MARCELLIN (*to* LAPINET, *indicating* ESTELLE). Shall we talk to her?

LAPINET (*with a comic sigh*). Oh, let's. Only I can't think how to begin. You know, once outside the Sorbonne, I'm not exactly ...

They go towards ESTELLE, *who had come downstage with* VALÉRIE, *while* CARLOTTA, *who has surged forth out of the shadows, calls out.*

CARLOTTA. Nearly eleven o'clock! Do you think anyone's thought about some lunch after the reading of the will? It's all very sad but it does make one peckish.

Without waiting for a reply, she has resumed her pacing with her stick, which is heard clicking on the tiled floor in the gloom throughout the rest of the scene.

MARCELLIN. Estelle dear, our good friend Lapinet would like to talk to you.

LAPINET (*cravenly*). To tell you the truth, Estelle, it was rather more our good friend Marcellin's idea than mine.

MARCELLIN (*giving him a stern look*). I'm always amazed, Lapinet, when I come across somebody more pusillanimous than me. (*He takes the plunge.*) We're uneasy, Estelle, very uneasy. We would like you, out of respect for Antoine's memory, to give us your word not to be too unwelcoming to that young woman.

ESTELLE (*stonily*). What do you want me to do – fling my arms round her neck?

MARCELLIN. We don't expect you to go that far, Estelle dear. Heroism has its limits. But Death has passed this way, obliterating many things. And I'm sure you realize how odious it would be if —

ESTELLE (*stonily*). Have *you* realized quite how odious it was to have her brought here?

MARCELLIN. Estelle, you know my discretion. I've never mentioned it, but I think I know that Antoine did genuinely love this young Maria Werner. You know how grave Antoine's neurosis had become. I'm his doctor, I was treating him for it, and I was very worried, I told you so at the time. That girl, although I smiled, like you at first, over the difference in their ages, certainly saved him from a very serious nervous collapse. She gave him, in fact, three years of peace. His last.

ESTELLE (*harshly*). And she left him to marry someone else. Leaving him alone to clean his guns.

MARCELLIN (*stands momentarily at a loss, then murmurs*). I think that was all agreed between them from the start.

ESTELLE. Including the cleaning of the gun?

VALÉRIE (*gently, from where she stands*). What do you most resent about the girl, Estelle – her being Antoine's last love or her leaving him to get married?

ESTELLE (*suddenly taut*). I longed passionately for three whole years for her to leave him! So he'd know the taste of it for once! (*She cries.*) Antoine cuckolded! At last!

VALÉRIE (*smiling*). That's an ugly word. It doesn't suit you. And it doesn't suit him.

CARLOTTA (*ringingly as she surges superbly out of the shadows*). I was unfaithful to him all the time! But I never made him a cuckold. It's a question of style. (*She adds, with a great, noble sweep of the arm.*) And repertoire!

One suddenly hears the characteristic sound of the motor outside, and frantic barking. The LAWYER *enters with a glass of water.*

LAWYER. The motor is here.

CARLOTTA (*surging from the shadows*). And my aspirin?

LAWYER (*handing her the glass*). And your aspirin, Madame. Excuse me.

He bows, clicks his heels and goes swiftly out. CARLOTTA *swallows her aspirin, growling.*

CARLOTTA. That's one the Prussians won't get! Funny, I can't think why, but their water's good!

A slack pause. All the characters have closed into groups. Enter the LAWYER, *preceding a charming little old lady, followed by a tall, shy young man and a tall, beautiful, impassive girl.* CRAVATAR *comes in last, chalky white, a handkerchief wound round his hand.*

LAWYER (*making the introductions*). Madame Duchemin and her son. Madame Staufenbach. Allow me to introduce Madame de St Flour, Madame Carlotta Alexandra, Madame Dubreuil and her daughter. Doctor Marcellin, Professor Lapinet.

OLD LADY (*exclaiming gaily*). Why, Rabbitskin! Haven't you got fat?

LAWYER (*turning*). And Monsieur Cravatar, drama critic of the *Gaulois.* Why, but you're hurt, sir?

CRAVATAR (*sombrely*). The dog bit me.

The dog howls outside. MARCELLIN *starts to giggle nervously, then freezes under* CRAVATAR'S *furious glare. Just then, a dull reverberating moan in the distance. The* LAWYER *gives a start, runs to the window, then goes out, pushing everybody aside with a muttered German oath. All the characters have moved aside, revealing the girl who remains alone upstage looking at* ESTELLE *who has not taken her eyes off her.*

MARCELLIN (*shoving everybody, panic stricken*). What was that, good God, what was that?

CRAVATAR (*who was one of the first at the window, swings round, fuming, and shouts*). That's it! This time we really are stuck! Antoine's brought it off again! Act One curtain! The avalanche! (*He yells, on the verge of hysteria.*) The bad taste! The hideous histrionic awfulness of it!

CARLOTTA (*delighted, rigidly upright on her stick, squealing*). Marvellous! Pure Euripides!

The dog has started howling again. CRAVATAR *pounces on his stick and rushes out. Everybody is at the windows, backs to the audience, save* ESTELLE *and the* GIRL *who stand looking at each other.* ANÉMONE, *who has turned round, looks at her too and murmurs.*

ANÉMONE. How beautiful she was . . .

ESTELLE (*in a dry small voice*). You think so?

Sudden blackout.

When the lights go up again a second later all the characters are sitting, backs to the audience, at the table, where the LAWYER *has taken his place. He is finishing the reading of the will. Beside him, on the table, a big phonograph with copper trumpet.*

LAWYER (*finishing the reading*). I appoint Herr Doctor Sigmund Munchlausen, my solicitor, to be executor of this my will and to watch over the accomplishment of my last wishes. Signed at Gerstorf, Bavaria, sound in mind and body. 12 July 1913. Antoine de St Flour.

There is a silent, gratified stir from all present, then a pause. At last CARLOTTA *says heavily and a little hoarsely.*

CARLOTTA. I'm not easily given to admiration, particularly not of my past lovers, but Antoine was a Medici. You aren't disappointed, Estelle, I imagine?

ESTELLE (*tersely*). I expected nothing from Antoine in that sphere. We were married under the law of equal property rights. He's been very generous.

CARLOTTA. And the royalties are and will remain considerable. Antoine has just entered the national repertoire. He will become a classic. What do you say, Cravatar?

CRAVATAR (*as marble*). Nothing.

CARLOTTA (*without emphasis, to the* LAWYER). But – this instrument . . . ?

LAWYER. I am coming to that. Monsieur de St Flour was – as I'm sure you know – a great lover of mechanical oddities. He was one of the first to have a telephone in this little backwater of ours – also the only motorized carriage anyone had ever seen in this corner of Bavaria. Among many other curiosities, Monsieur de St Flour also had – and he derived great amusement from it in his lonely evenings – this phonograph here and a vast collection of cylinders. Odd songs, monologues and recordings of classical plays. We have here the famous English clown George Robey, Mademoiselle Mistinguett and even a recording of Madame Sarah Bernhardt in Hamlet. If these little pieces would amuse you they are of course at your disposal.

CARLOTTA (*grouchily*). Too kind. But I haven't come a thousand kilometres with my rheumatism to listen to the trumpetings of Madame Sarah Bernhardt.

LAWYER (*with a smile*). I thought not, but this cylinder here is sure to interest you. In his last days, Monsieur de St Flour had conceived the project of recording certain things himself, poems he liked, certain scenes from his plays —

CARLOTTA. But how could he possibly do that here?

LAWYER. When the fancy took him, nothing was impossible to Monsieur de St Flour! He persuaded – at great cost I may say – a recording engineer from Munich to trail all the way up here with the necessary equipment . . . I was myself present at this recording session, and most interesting it was too, from a scientific point of view. And at the end of it, having asked us all to

leave him, Monsieur de St Flour conceived the idea of recording a little message for you all – as if he could already foresee his
death and your visit here. If you allow, I shall now set the instrument in motion and leave you to listen to it alone. You will note,
with some emotion I fancy, how the brilliance of this modern
age has in some fashion superseded death. It is Monsieur de
St Flour's very own voice, scarcely distorted, which this
mechanical device will reproduce for you. There. I shall
insert the cylinder. The main thing is to get the axis exactly
vertical . . . It's all in working order. When I have left the
room, perhaps one of the gentlemen will be so kind as to
move this lever – so – to the right . . . I shall now withdraw.
(*He bows and goes.*)

CARLOTTA. It's very moving. And how like him, the whole idea!
There was an incurable practical joker in Antoine. Shall we
listen to it – are you all willing?

> ESTELLE *sits rigidly, without saying a word.* VALÉRIE *comes
> to her side and says, kindly.*

VALÉRIE. I'm right beside you, Estelle.

ESTELLE (*stiffly*). Thank you, Valérie, but I can hear Antoine's
voice one more time without falling into a faint.

CARLOTTA. Right then, Lapinet, off you go! It's prodigiously
moving. Wait a second. Let me settle my leg.

> LAPINET, *a little scared, bends over the instrument and gingerly
> operates the lever as if in danger of getting an electric shock. A
> scratching noise and then suddenly a song of Mistinguett's
> blares out, cracked, and eerie. Everyone sits up, startled. There
> is a small wave of panic.*

(*Shouting.*) Stop the thing, stop it! It's scandalous!

LAPINET (*wildly*). I can't, I don't know how!

> MARCELLIN *has rushed to the door just as the* LAWYER *enters,
> red with embarrassment, while Mistinguett is still screeching
> gaily on the gramophone.*

LAWYER. I do beg your pardon! That was inexcusable. It was the wrong cylinder! I did label them all so carefully, but the maid must have mixed them up when she was dusting. I am truly grieved. (*He has stopped the instrument.*) Ah, here we are. This is it. I can't apologize enough, ladies ...

CARLOTTA (*grunting*). We all make mistakes.

LAWYER (*stiffly*). Not a German lawyer! Just press this, monsieur, if you would. (*He clicks his heels, bows and goes out.*)

LAPINET. Shall I?

CARLOTTA. Go on.

> *A pause, a loud crackle first and then at last one hears* ANTOINE's *voice, nonchalant and deep.*

ANTOINE'S VOICE. Hullo, friends. First of all, let me thank you for coming out here, especially if it's in winter. I hope it isn't snowing too hard.

> CARLOTTA *gives a savage growl. The voice goes on.*

ANTOINE'S VOICE. Thank you, Estelle. I can see you in my mind's eye, all frail and small, and looking a little pale. I'm sure your grief is great, but I know that you look your best in black. Thank you, Carlotta and Valérie. Thank you, Anémone. I shall ask to have you sent for too. Are you beautiful? Are you grown up? Are you already married? After all, one doesn't die to order and I don't know exactly when you'll be listening to this. Thank you, Lapinet, you good-natured fellow, for hoisting your professorial paunch up to this altitude, so far away from the Sorbonne, you who hate nature anywhere outside the Georgics of Virgil. This is the last dirty trick I'll ever play on you. Thank you, Marcellin, my too kind-hearted, too frivolous friend. And forgive me for dying at other hands but yours. But it's better I did. It would certainly have spoilt your evening to have to admit, over your friend's body, to the ineffectiveness of your doctoring.

> *A short patch of crackle, then the voice goes on, more inwardly.*

I thank you too, Gabrielle. I imagine your husband must be old enough now – and you too – to allow you this little jaunt. Thank you for coming with your son to their weird gathering – where once again I shan't turn up – like at our last rendezvous in the gardens of the Luxembourg so long ago. Thank you and forgive me.

A little pause. The voice goes on.

Are you there too, Maria? I hope you were able to come, and I hope they didn't snarl at you too much. Are you still as beautiful? Have you had your child?

A pause, then the voice goes on.

There. I don't think there's anyone I've forgotten. Oh yes! I asked Meyer ages ago to send you to my obsequies, so I should get a good review from you at last! Are you there, Cravatar?

They all turn slightly to CRAVATAR *and then suddenly a chill of terror runs through them, for the phonograph goes on, nasally, implacably —*

PHONOGRAPH. Are you there, Cravatar? Are you there, Cravatar? Are you there, Cravatar? Are you there, Cravatar? Are you there, Cravatar?

CRAVATAR (*leaping to his feet and yelling*). Stop that thing! Stop it!

LAPINET (*wildly*). I don't know how it works!

MARCELLIN has dashed to the door once again. The LAWYER rushes in, while the phonograph goes on — Are you there, Cravatar? Are you there, Cravatar? Are you there, Cravatar? At last the LAWYER stops the instrument.

LAWYER (*covered in confusion*). A technical hitch! This machine isn't working quite as it should. I'll just move the needle along the cylinder a little bit.

He replaces the needle carefully. There is a very painful

c

scratching, while the cylinder regains speed. Then we hear ANTOINE'S *voice again, still very distorted.*

ANTOINE'S VOICE. But I know that deep down you've always hated me.

CRAVATAR *moves away a little and nervously lights a cigarette.*

(*Normal now.*) There. I wanted to bring you together – even you, Cravatar – because you have been the characters in my life. Life always seems like a three-ring circus because there's a lot of noise and bustle and walk-ons milling about. But at the end of it, you come to see that there were only four or five performers and that the play was a secret one, hidden away behind so many spurious theatrical effects. I know there's a certain tastelessness in collecting you all here. I could after all have left you whatever I planned to leave you through my lawyer in Paris. I've always had a streak of bad taste – which was incidentally the ruination of my play-writing, isn't that so, Cravatar? But life's in bad taste too, and so is death . . . On doing my accounts – although I've always been so preoccupied with other people's troubles, basically, that my life has sometimes been restricted by it, I think on reflection that I never gave you very much. In any case, you all complained exorbitantly about me. Living is very difficult and honesty almost impossible. But every human being has his secret and it may be that under the unretouched character that each one of you insisted I should play – I had my secret too. Think about that for a moment if you can – as you're all here – to kill time, which is so hard to kill and yet so short – while you wait together for the train from Munich. And after that – hooray for Paris and forgetfulness. It's a charming city, Paris, and a good place to live in and I long for it sometimes. Today, as I talk to you, it's mild and sunny, it's summertime. The flowers in the garden are insolently beautiful and this late afternoon is heavy with scent . . . they've just mown the lawn . . . Only all this happiness is no use to me, because I am alone.

I know, Estelle, it was my own doing! I've been living alone for four months now, not opening my mouth except to order my dinner in German, a language I shall positively never be able to learn. And it's an abominable thing, being alone. As somebody once said, I forget who – one's in bad company . . .

Only the crackling is heard now. The LAWYER *stops the machine and says simply.*

LAWYER. The recording stops there. I had to play it through first, as Monsieur de St Flour forgot to tell me which cylinder it was on. The rest of it consists of songs he was fond of, happy songs . . .

A heavy silence. Nobody moves for a while, except CRAVATAR *who has got up and is pacing nervously back and forth upstage. Suddenly the dog starts to howl.* CRAVATAR *seizes a stick and flings out, fuming. Another motionless silence, then* MARIA, *who had been sitting in the back row, a little apart, gets up without a word and goes off up the stairs at the back of the room. The others, still shaken by their recent experience, turn to look at her in mild surprise.*

CARLOTTA (*hoarsely*). Where is she going?
ESTELLE (*bitterly*). Up to the bedrooms I imagine. She knows where they are.

A brief awkward pause, then CARLOTTA *rises and exclaims baldly.*

CARLOTTA. Right. Who's the mistress of the house here? Very confusing it all is. Has anybody seen to that snack? I'm feeling empty.
LAWYER. I took the liberty of seeing to all that myself. Fortunately there are plenty of provisions here. The housekeeper has prepared a cold buffet luncheon in the dining-hall. Excuse me. I think it might be ready now. (*He goes quickly out.*)
CARLOTTA (*rising painfully*). Well, let's go then. After a funeral

those that are left alive have something to eat. That's a law as old as death. Give me a hand, Marcellin, my left leg is set rigid. God knows what uneatable muck they'll cram down our throats in the next two days. Barbarians!

MARCELLIN (*going out with her*). And here am I with a highly important session at the Academy of Medicine on Friday!

CARLOTTA. Has something new cropped up, in medicine?

MARCELLIN. Yes. We're blackballing Chantepierre. He's had the gall to put himself up for election.

CARLOTTA. The man who conquered typhus?

MARCELLIN (*crisply*). He conquered typhus, but he was with Zola over Dreyfus. The man's a cad.

They go out, GABRIELLE DUCHEMIN *has taken* LAPINET's *arm.*

GABRIELLE. I'll sit next to you, Lapinet, may I? I don't know a soul here. Do you know, my eldest son is studying for his master's degree in letters, just like you. And the other one has just got into the School of Military Engineering. He's got his father's gift for mathematics . . . Do you remember how you used to club together with Antoine to buy me dinner in the Latin Quarter? Oh, Rabbitskin, Rabbitskin, you used to be so slim! Whatever did you do to yourself?

LAPINET (*pitifully*). I don't know, really.

They go out. ESTELLE *has not moved.* VALÉRIE *goes to her.*

VALÉRIE. Aren't you coming, Estelle?

ESTELLE. I'm not hungry. And I certainly don't feel like sitting down at that table.

VALÉRIE. We're stranded here for two days, you'll have to eat *something*.

ESTELLE. I don't see why.

VALÉRIE. That's absurd. Come on.

ESTELLE. No.

VALÉRIE *gives a little shrug and goes out with* ANÉMONE.
ESTELLE *remains alone, in her black dress, stiffly upright in her chair.* CRAVATAR *comes bursting in and asks.*

CRAVATAR. Where is everybody?

ESTELLE. Eating. They're hungry.

CRAVATAR. What a fandango! It's abominable.

ESTELLE. Abominable. But he wanted it this way. That was the joker in him, as Carlotta says. Fancy getting that common little woman here – and that boy who looks so indecently like him, the bad taste of it!

CRAVATAR. Antoine was full to the gills with bad taste. He loathed me, that we know, but to go and make that grotesque outburst on this ridiculous contraption – when he was good and dead! (*He cries out, seething.*) And I can't even fling a glove in his face and drag him out at dawn to stick a bit of cold steel through his ribs! I should have done it long ago. I had cause enough ten times over. (*He paces about a bit more then stops and adds dully.*) No, it's not true. I didn't always hate him. He just annoyed me, that's all, with his grand airs, and he annoyed everybody else come to that. He made enemies of all his fellow cadets at the Military Academy, with that everlasting smile of his. He didn't make the grade, incidentally. He passed out as cavalry sergeant, despite pretty good marks in mathematics. All because the Corps Commander was like the rest of us – he simply couldn't stand him.

ESTELLE. I think he liked being hated. Even when he played for sympathy with his unhappy little boy act.

CRAVATAR (*seething*). Well, that's one thing he managed to bring off, then. It's a sad thing to say, but there are a good many I know in Paris, who heaved a sigh of relief, I can tell you.

ESTELLE, *cold as marble, says nothing.* CRAVATAR *paces about a bit, fuming, then he goes to her and says abruptly.*

Estelle, I never told you this, but I only really began to hate him when I saw what he was doing to you.

ESTELLE (*unforthcoming*). I know. You've been very pleasant to me always.

CRAVATAR. A fine person like you, Estelle, extinguished by that bastard!

ESTELLE (*strangely*). Poor Estelle! A little snuffed-out candle.

CRAVATAR. When so many other men would have been more than glad to — (*He adds.*) Well, anyhow, you're free now.

ESTELLE. Yes.

CRAVATAR (*after a pause*). I've admired your absurd fidelity, against all comers, in that little Parisian world where nobody bothers too much with scruples of that sort. I could see that you were very much sought after.

ESTELLE (*quietly*). Yes. It's funny. I was attractive to everybody except the man I married.

CRAVATAR (*pursuing his train of thought*). We all know about womanizers, Paris is crawling with them. But to begin with, they do it with some style, when they care to be thought of as men of the world. And then again, they usually marry wives who pay them back in kind. Nobody could ever understand your reserve.

ESTELLE. Nobody. Not even I.

CRAVATAR. But, dammit, you were in love with him once, weren't you?

ESTELLE. At twenty, when he took me from my father's house, yes, very much.

CRAVATAR. And you did have —

ESTELLE (*finishing his sentence with a tense little smile*). – what they call a few marvellous years . . . While he was giving me my children.

CRAVATAR. Was he unfaithful even then?

ESTELLE. If he was I never knew it. He always lived in the country. It was a period when he did a lot of writing.

CRAVATAR. And were you happy?

ESTELLE. Yes. Behind a fog. To be quite honest I think I was a little bored.

CRAVATAR. People thought you sad even then, when they came out to see you in that big house you had. Why didn't you come back to Paris? Walks through the woods are all very nice but they soon pall.

ESTELLE. Antoine always seemed to shine so in public, but basically he adored that house and the solitude of it. And Antoine's life, when you come to examine it, consisted of houses and nothing else. He chose that one to herald in his docile young girl-wife and his newly minted desire for a family, after the hell of Carlotta, that's all. The house and I were part of the same lot. Anyway, he seemed very happy. That happiness – a little muted for me, I must say – lasted a few years and then . . . (*She stops.*)

CRAVATAR. And then?

ESTELLE. Then it stopped being happiness quite . . . Quarrels found their way into the house. Soft footed at first, fairly unassuming, like strange ladies a little unsure of their welcome – and then triumphant. In the end, *they* were at home in the fine house, not us.

CRAVATAR. What a funny way of putting it.

ESTELLE. Yes. Poor Estelle – she's noted for it – has a sense of humour. It's served her well in her new career as a bitch.

CRAVATAR. You aren't a bitch.

ESTELLE (*dully*). I am. I've turned into one. For ten years I've resented everyone.

CRAVATAR. For what?

ESTELLE (*after a brief hesitation*). For my not being me.

CRAVATAR. What do you mean?

ESTELLE (*with a sudden harsh cry*). I've never been me! I've been Antoine's wife. And now, if I'm not careful, I'll be Antoine's widow. That's why I started to resent him. That's why I pitted myself against him, over everything, all the time, with an aggressiveness he simply couldn't understand. Why I insisted on coming back to Paris, why I began going out with everyone, on my own, whenever he didn't want to go, just in order to be me, at last. (*She repeats.*) Me! Me! I exist, you know! Antoine isn't the only human being on earth!

ANÉMONE *has come in.*

ANÉMONE (*gently*). He isn't even there at all now, Estelle, if you want to know.

A pause. Then ESTELLE *asks truculently.*

ESTELLE. Did you want something, Anémone?

ANÉMONE. Mother sent me to ask you to come in to luncheon. She thinks it would look better if you did. If only for that German lawyer, who's standing to attention behind his chair. He'll never be persuaded to sit down to eat without you.

ESTELLE (*in a light, dry tone as she rises*). Very well, let's go. We must be merciful to German lawyers who are paralysed with politeness.

ANÉMONE (*in a strange, gentle voice*). We must be merciful to everyone, Estelle.

ESTELLE (*with a little laugh*). How wise we are these days at eighteen. In my time all we thought about was having fun. Coming, Cravatar?

They go out. ANÉMONE *has remained alone beside the phonograph. Her hand hovers a little over the switch, then she starts the machine and tries to find a passage on the cylinder. She succeeds and* ANTOINE's *voice is heard saying softly.*

ANTOINE'S VOICE. Thank you, Anémone. I shall ask for you to be sent for too. Are you beautiful? Are you grown up? Are you married already? After all, one doesn't die to order and I don't know exactly when you will be listening to this . . .

She stops the cylinder. She moves her hand with a kind of light, tender caress on the big copper trumpet and says softly, standing very still.

ANÉMONE. I'm here. I'm not married and I think I look prettier than I did. You wouldn't touch me because I was too young, but I shall always love you. And all that money you left me I shall send to Dr Schweizer, and I'll go to him in Africa to care for the lepers. And when I'm very very old . . .

She stops. She stands very still, full of a childlike resolve which should make one smile. The YOUNG MAN *has come in. He says awkwardly.*

YOUNG MAN. Mademoiselle, I've been sent to fetch you.

ANÉMONE *looks at him, hostile at first and then surprised to see him so charming and so ill at ease. The look lasts just a little too long, one feels. She gives a little smile. He too. Then she says simply.*

ANÉMONE. I'm coming.

She goes, he follows her silently. The curtain falls.

Act Two

When the curtain goes up, it is still snowing. There is no telling what the time is, doubtless late afternoon. CRAVATAR *is at the window, upstage looking out into the courtyard.*

GABRIELLE *and* LAPINET *are sitting together on the sofa.* GABRIELLE *is working at a faintly absurd bit of embroidery.*

LAPINET. That frightful fecklessness of Antoine's . . .

GABRIELLE (*firmly*). Now don't start that again, Lapinet, saying nasty things about him, like in the old days when you were jealous. Antoine was very goodhearted. I never met any man as kind as he was. Only he was forgetful. It happens. I brought up my son, I married a very decent man and I lived my life just the same.

LAPINET (*bitterly*). And I became an old potbellied academic.

GABRIELLE (*smiling*). And you forgot me . . . Love dies, you know, Rabbitskin.

LAPINET (*heavily*). Alas.

GABRIELLE (*with a comic little cry*). You mean, thank goodness. It's a dreadful accident to have, and you must count yourself lucky if you get away with all four limbs intact.

LAPINET (*heavily again, after a pause*). Intact for what?

A little pause, then GABRIELLE *says, tonelessly too.*

GABRIELLE. Not much, it's true. The little daily round of life, like an ant. But when you gamble everlastingly on love, like Antoine, look what happens, you end up in the same wilderness. What have we been doing, all of us, ever since this morning? Waiting until they clear the avalanche, that's all. Great tall Carlotta on her stick, little Estelle in her black veils, lovely Valérie – and even silly doting Gabrielle Dusmesnil here – who'd have flung herself at a word from him, hand in hand with him into the river, she loved him so much – what are they doing, all those enamoured women, Rabbitskin, can you tell me? Counting the shovelfuls as the Bavarians work away down there. And Antoine's mouth, that they kissed so often, turn and turn about, is shapeless already in his handsome rotting coffin. There are plenty of beautiful poems about that in those fine books of yours. And it isn't that sad, Rabbitskin. Stuff to teach to schoolboys, that's about all.

LAPINET (*with a sudden cry, comic and despairing*). I did so want to be loved by you, Gabrielle, and become a great poet!

GABRIELLE (*rising and laughing at the idea*). Rabbitskin! You explain poets to the young, that's already something! (*She asks, in a different tone of voice, tidying away her needlework.*) Where are Alexander and that little girl? The lawyer found them some snow-shoes and they haven't been seen since.

LAPINET. They're roaming the mountain-side. Oh to be twenty and running across the snow with a girl!

GABRIELLE (*still laughing*). Too late, Rabbitskin, you'd sink right in, however big your snow-shoes.

CARLOTTA *and* MARCELLIN *come in from outside, white with snow and all muffled up.*

CARLOTTA. We went out for a breath of air. It's unendurable and boring both. Snow, snow, and snow again. What can you see? Nothing. Typical. When they do happen to have some scenery worth looking at, they make quite certain you can't see it!

MARCELLIN. The air has a tang, very healthy.

CARLOTTA (*growling*). It's clear you haven't got asthma, man. We spied out the cemetery up on the hillside, it's between the house and the village. I'll tell you one thing, I certainly can't get up that far without a lift!

LAPINET. The weather may improve by tomorrow.

CARLOTTA. The weather possibly, but not my knee. I know it, I'll be stiff as a board for a month. Oh, very bright of me it was, accepting this invitation!

They look at her a little embarrassed, as she carries straight on.

Yes, I know. Antoine's dead – and he died at the beginning of winter. Why couldn't he have died in the summer, that would have suited everybody. Bavaria must be very pretty in summer. Lots of little flowers everywhere. Marcellin, you know the language, go and ask that old housekeeper what that drink was she gave me after lunch. It quite perked me up. Was she Antoine's servant, when he was alive?

MARCELLIN. Yes. And the lawyer told me something very touching. It seems she was his nursemaid long ago and he came across her and took her back into his service in his last days – you know – Frida! He was always talking about her. He can't not have mentioned her to you.

CARLOTTA (*setting herself on to the sofa, grunting*). Can't recall. It was theatre we talked about mostly with Antoine, when we weren't quarrelling, that is.

LAPINET (*sidling up, greedily*). What's that, Marcellin? The woman who waited at table, is she the celebrated Frida? Why, that's very interesting, from the biographical point of view. I'd go so far as to say it's a pearl! Could you talk to her for me, Marcellin? The woman must know some amazing details about him. I've already collected a fair amount of childhood photographs and in most of them there she is, this breathtaking blonde girl in Bavarian costume. (*Winking.*) Antoine's first love, at eight years old, what?

MARCELLIN (*vaguely ribald*). And nothing left of it all, alas, but the costume. So tell me, you're preparing your little booklet on him already, are you, you ghoul? True, in the publishing world you have to strike while the iron's . . . I almost said hot.

LAPINET (*annoyed*). Your taproom jokes amuse no one but yourself, Marcellin. I was Antoine's friend, I have a vast personal documentation and access to family papers. You don't expect me to stand by while Cravatar writes the book, do you?

CRAVATAR (*stepping up*). Who's taking my name in vain?

LAPINET. Oh, you're still there, are you, glued to your window? What have you been at ever since lunch?

CRAVATAR (*darkly*). Watching the dog. His kennel is right below here. Ever since the larruping I gave him, so long as he sees me watching, he doesn't dare howl. I'm sick of the sound of him, histrionic brute!

CARLOTTA (*crying from upstage*). Marcellin, you're forgetting me! I need a little topping up.

MARCELLIN. I'll see to it right away.

LAPINET (*following him*). I'll come with you. I'm rather keen to see this Frida at close quarters. The whole of Antoine's childhood – imagine!

They go out.

CRAVATAR (*going to* CARLOTTA). What did you think of that speech of Antoine's, on that machine?

CARLOTTA. I didn't catch it all. I was sitting a bit far away. But I found it very touching.

CRAVATAR. As a professional, did you think he put it over well?

CARLOTTA. Very.

CRAVATAR (*bitterly*). Too well. I should think he rehearsed it in front of a mirror. I can just see him working out a way to tear our hearts out. He adored making people feel guilty and he was an expert at it too. It's amazing the number of people he hooked that way. 'Poor Antoine, here am I dead – and you're still alive – and you never loved me as you should have done.' That was his Jewish side.

CARLOTTA. But Antoine wasn't a Jew!

CRAVATAR (*seething*). No, but he should have been! Oh, he was past master at making people cry. That's how he got all his women. Anyway, that was his stock in trade. He'd drawn tears from the gallery for so long, he knew exactly how to set about it.

If I know anything about him, he must have sworn to catch us in the net for one last time with his party trick. Anyway, it fell flat as a pancake with me.

CARLOTTA (*suddenly*). You wear me out with your hatred, Cravatar. We're snowed up in the heart of Bavaria and my knee hurts. The situation is painful enough as it is, I don't feel like listening to you spewing out your venom into the bargain. My health isn't good enough to quarrel any more. Why don't you make yourself useful instead? Go back and stand guard over the dog.

> CRAVATAR *goes icily back to his window.* CARLOTTA *looks at* GABRIELLE *who has been staring at her intently for a while. She cries out suddenly.*

CARLOTTA. And what are *you* staring at pray?

GABRIELLE. I'm making up for lost time. There were photographs of you of course, but for years and years a sort of modesty prevented me from going back to the Comédie Française. And in the early days, when sleep didn't come easy, I spent my nights trying to imagine you.

CARLOTTA (*grunting*). Whatever for, when you could see me for the price of a loaf? Everybody can see me for the price of a loaf.

GABRIELLE. I told you, the first few years, I'd have felt ashamed at going to peep at you. Then later, when the pain grew a little less sharp, I let curiosity get the better of me and I went to see you – for two francs actually – by queuing all night for the gallery.

CARLOTTA (*arrogantly*). So you saw me. And how far did that get you?

GABRIELLE. I thought you very beautiful – terrifying too. That evening you were playing Hermione. I was suddenly aware of my own insignificance, and I understood Antoine.

CARLOTTA (*grumbling*). The reaction of a young goose! Never understand your enemy. That's always the way to lose a war.

GABRIELLE (*gently*). But you weren't my enemy.

CARLOTTA. Yes, I was, I'd taken something away from you.

Never let anyone take anything away from you – ever. Look at me, when he lost his head over Estelle – and yet God knows we'd knocked about a bit, both of us. I had a young friend at the time, whom I was very fond of – a small-part actor in the company. He's one of the stars now, Ducourmu – you may have seen his Nero last year. I pretended to accept the situation – it suited my plans at the time, but I took care to make life impossible for both of them. Crammed with incident, their honeymoon was, I can promise you. I committed suicide three times.

GABRIELLE. What – properly?

CARLOTTA (*grunting*). Well, enough to drag him back three times from Florence on his bridal trip. It would have paid him to get a season ticket. I wasn't as wretched as all that, to tell the truth, but I wanted *him* to be. That's love for you. Mark you, I paid the price each time. Young Estelle chewed her fingernails all alone in her bridal suite, he spent the night on the train, riddled with remorse – but I had to do the vomiting.

GABRIELLE (*gently*). I didn't commit suicide. I got married.

CARLOTTA (*gloomily*). It comes to the same thing.

A pause, then she cries suddenly.

Suppose we're stuck here, you aren't going to stare at me like that for three whole days, are you? What do you want, my autograph?

GABRIELLE (*still looking at her strangely*). I'm looking at my pain as a young girl and it's doing me good. There's something rather amusing about it. So that's all the heartbreak amounted to. It was only you. An old theatrical monster.

CARLOTTA (*arrogant*). If you want us to act like fishwives, my good girl, I'm game. But I've had more training – you'll never stand up to me. It's not all sweetness and light in the theatre, you know. When it comes to mud-slinging, we're athletes at the Comédie! And not just in mud-slinging – in florentine bitchery – the polite kind, the genuine article, the one that knocks your good woman out for life. So don't you tweak the old lion's tail. We're all tired out and we've come here to have a little weep over Antoine who's kicked the bucket. (*She adds desperately.*) If only my knee didn't hurt so.

> GABRIELLE *looks at the old woman moaning pitifully as she rubs her knee and asks suddenly.*

GABRIELLE. Have you tried Brahmin's Balm?

CARLOTTA. No. What's that?

GABRIELLE. An old remedy. The label says it's a secret Hindu formula. It's the only thing that gives me any relief when I get stiff. In a couple of hours, that's it, I'm on my feet again.

CARLOTTA. Which knee is it, with you?

GABRIELLE. The right.

CARLOTTA. Mine's the left. That's even more bloody.

GABRIELLE. Why?

CARLOTTA (*irritably*). I don't know! Because that's the one that hurts! And it eases it, does it, that Hindu stuff of yours?

GABRIELLE. Quick as quick. I've got some in my suitcase. I'll get it for you, shall I? I'll give you a little rub.

CARLOTTA (*suddenly touched*). You're a lamb – yes, go on, do. We women have to help each other. Men are all pigs, that's for sure. (*She looks at her suddenly, almost human.*) And he left you, my little lamb, expecting his child, to come and prance attendance on me backstage, and tell me he was mad about me?

GABRIELLE (*kindly*). Yes, but he didn't know I was pregnant ... I'm sure if he had, he'd —

CARLOTTA. Even so! A fine piece of muck, he was, your Antoine. But don't you worry, I paid him back for you. You got your revenge, I saw to that.

GABRIELLE (*asking with a kind of anguished shyness*). You can't mean you never loved him, can you?

CARLOTTA (*dully*). No, of course I don't. When you're unfaithful to a man for ten years it means you love him, otherwise you leave him. And he *was* a marvellous lover. As maddening as

nettlerash, not all that intelligent, but still, he had something ...
Now run along and fetch me your ointment, there's a love, and
I'll tell you all about it while you rub my knee. It'll help kill
time.

GABRIELLE. Right. But I don't know that I really want to have
you tell me about Antoine ...

CARLOTTA. My dear, it's all so long ago! It's the Count of Monte
Cristo. An old novel that gives nobody the shivers any more.
We know the story backwards and we know it all comes right
in the end.

GABRIELLE (*quietly*). Not for Antoine.

CARLOTTA (*sombrely, with a wave of the hand*). Pooh. At our age,
it's the retreat from Moscow. You stop weeping over the fallen
comrade, because you've at last realized that we're all going the
same way.

A pause.

And it's still snowing! German swine!

*She goes on muttering indistinguishably, an old effigy, bolt
upright on her cane.* GABRIELLE *looks at her again for a second
with that sad puzzlement she has shown throughout the scene,
then she goes out. On her way she passes* MARCELLIN *who has
come in, followed by a very old woman in Bavarian costume
ceremoniously carrying a glass on a tray, which she offers to*
CARLOTTA.

MARCELLIN. Here's your posset.

CARLOTTA (*with a gruesome accent*). Dankeschön Darling. Is that
right, Marcellin?

OLD WOMAN. Bitteschön.

*She goes out, inscrutable and silent under the others' intrigued
gaze.*

LAPINET (*who has been staring at her avidly, murmurs as soon as she
has gone*). It's prodigious!

D

CARLOTTA (*drinking her drink*). What is?

LAPINET. That woman. The whole of Antoine's childhood. It brings tears to my eyes. I wish I could take her back to Paris!

CARLOTTA (*grunting into her glass*). You don't have to go that far. Antoine was a howling baby once, all right – so were we all. We've all done our messes in little potties and sucked lollipops and we've all had nurserymaids – but it wouldn't enter anyone's head to turn them into museum pieces.

LAPINET. But dear friend, in the present case —

CARLOTTA (*cutting in, furious*). No! It gets on my nerves this modern fetish for digging out the petty details of a great man's life, when the great things he has done, nobody really cares two pins about. Antoine was a great playwright and he wrote some very fine plays. Right. That's all there is to it. Let them revive a few. The rest is eyewash. (*She drains her glass, coughing.*) Not bad this grog, but it's stiff stuff.

MARCELLIN. And I shouldn't think it'll do your knee much good!

CARLOTTA (*to* MARCELLIN). No, Doctor, but it's good for the stomach, and that's where it gets to first. (*She goes on, furious.*) You're an academic, Lapinet – right through to the bone! Molière didn't even leave a single manuscript. Those fellows didn't save them up for posterity, like the self-important little runts of our day. They wrote on lavatory paper and once they'd sent them to the copyists they wrapped their fried potatoes in them. *They* were men. Racine, same thing. Racine is my God. But if they found his false teeth, do you think I'd cross the street to see them? That's stuff for Milady Bernhardt who exhibits herself in circuses. It's mighty Barnum.

LAPINET (*at last getting a word in*). Yes, of course, dear friend, but in this present case, it's legitimate to feel that there is something moving at seeing, in flesh and blood, a person who was – this I know – Antoine's whole security, his whole universe as a child. Antoine always kept a deep impression of his neglected childhood. And his nurse – this Frida – was for a long time the great and only love of his life. I know it's a very modern theory, and highly controversial, but it appears provable that there remains, deep in one's subconscious —

CARLOTTA (*growling*). What's that?

LAPINET. Deep in the most secret part of ourselves, if you like – an indelible trace of our earliest emotions, and his love for this woman – this maid – who replaced his pleasure-seeking mother, did most certainly leave its stamp on Antoine.

CARLOTTA (*cackling*). That must be why he slept with all of mine then, the hog! You couldn't ring for tea of an afternoon, but up he'd get, in that casual way he had, and phwt – the second tea was served, he'd wedge the girl behind the door. I got a Chinese valet in the end, so as to drink my tea in peace.

CRAVATAR (*who has come back to them, eyes aglint*). How very interesting! I knew nothing of his ancillary tastes. No doubt about it, one learns something fresh every day about our friend.

CARLOTTA (*grouchily*). There's a lot more besides that I could say about Antoine – but not to you, Cravatar. You'd be far too delighted.

CRAVATAR (*amicably*). Pooh! We're old Parisians, dear friend. And underneath their high-toned conformism, I must say the sexual comportment of my contemporaries has always interested me prodigiously. Lift a corner of the veil and you go from surprise to surprise. I always thought of our late friend as a vigorous man, certainly, he abundantly proved it! – But basically, in that particular sphere, I'd have called him fairly straightforward. A man with vices, was he – our handsome Antoine, a man of complications?

CARLOTTA (*superbly*). I don't know what you call vices, Cravatar, I only know about tastes! And pleasure is always complicated. If only because it takes two of you.

MARCELLIN. What you tell us, dear diva, gives us the basic key to Antoine. Doesn't his somewhat tumultuous emotional life reflect quite simply his deep desire – always thwarted no doubt– to be one of a pair? Antoine was alone and every time he changed companions he was hoping he would stop being alone. When he parted from that last girl – in circumstances that we'll probably never know – he found himself old, worn out, back in his childhood loneliness again. And he was no doubt unable to endure it.

CRAVATAR (*with a slightly unhealthy curiosity*). Marcellin, you were his closest friend – what did that girl mean to him, exactly? You can tell us now! We only caught a glimpse of her this morning. Then she vanished into the upper floors. She's a beauty, yes, but there's a peasant look about her. And nothing in her appearance would seem to warrant —

MARCELLIN. I never saw Antoine again after his retirement to Germany. A few letters for things he needed done in Paris, when he barely spoke of her, just mentioning her name as if it was an understood thing. What about you, Lapinet?

LAPINET. Everything I ever knew about her I got from you, my good old lad. It was even you who told me she existed.

CRAVATAR (*aquiver*). Isn't there a hint of a mystery in all this, something it would be interesting to unearth – after all, we were his friends and everything that affects Antoine affects us too. I must say his abrupt withdrawal from society – when outside his periods of creativity he was the most Parisian of us all – has always struck me as very strange. Hasn't it you?

MARCELLIN. The only one who can know that is the lawyer. But he's giving nothing away. He's a locked man. With a padlock stamped 'made in Germany' – the unbreakable kind.

> ESTELLE *and* VALÉRIE *come in, muffled up and covered in snow, followed by the* LAWYER.

VALÉRIE. You shouldn't have turned back so soon, Carlotta. The village is really beautiful, you can see it from the top of the road. And there's one plucky little ant working away on the avalanche. She's cleared half of it already.

LAWYER. Monsieur de St Flour was very fond of this village. He stayed there for two weeks in his old servants' house, before he even thought of buying this place.

ESTELLE (*suddenly*). You mean he came here alone, to begin with?

LAWYER. Yes, Madame. Monsieur de St Flour arrived one night, alone, at Frida's, whom he hadn't seen since childhood. Naturally, he couldn't expect the kind of comfort he was used to, in that little peasant's cottage, nor could he settle down to a routine of work there. So after a few days he paid me a visit, in my chambers, which is how I came to have the honour of making his acquaintance. He expressed his desire to settle in our part of the world and he asked me if this residence, which had stood empty for years, was up for sale. I wrote, without much hope, to the owners as I knew it was a family seat – but certain complications in the line of succession made them decide to accept Monsieur de St Flour's offer – which was, I may say, substantial.

ESTELLE. And he came to live up here, alone?

LAWYER (*a little stiffly*). After a brief period for renovations and redecorating, yes, Madame, alone, with Frida, whom he took back into his employ.

A pause. Everyone would like to ask a question, nobody does. At last ESTELLE *takes the plunge, and says, a little dryly, a little disagreeably as always.*

ESTELLE. You aren't in any way obliged to answer this, Monsieur, but I think, after the reading of my husband's will, that a good many things could now be called open secrets. When did that young person come to live here?

LAWYER (*after a short hesitation*). Some few months later, Madame. Frida, feeling herself to be a little too old to undertake this big house on her own asked her niece, the then Fräulein Werner, to come and help her run it.

A pause. He adds stiffly.

Incidentally, I have to tell you that Madame Staufenbach, her presence here being no longer necessary, borrowed some snowshoes at the farm and set off over the mountain-side to try to bypass the avalanche. She knows the terrain well; she will have reached the village by this afternoon, where she will take the mail coach early tomorrow for Munich.

ESTELLE (*acidly, after a pause*). She's deprived me of a great pleasure. In fact, she only came for whatever belongings she couldn't take away the last time. Or a little memento of her amorous escapade, perhaps?

> *The* LAWYER *has turned to ice. There is a disapproving silence at these words. Only* CRAVATAR *cackles, upstage, where he is still pacing about.* VALÉRIE *gives a pained sigh.*

VALÉRIE. Estelle. I know you're nicer than your resentment makes you sound. But not everyone here knows that. Stealing the teaspoons! Now really! You sound just like your mother.

LAWYER (*stiffly*). I must ask you to excuse me. I am standing in as Hausfrau, as we say in our country and I must give orders for dinner.

> *He bows, tight as a clam and goes out.*

CARLOTTA (*tetchily*). The German padlock has snapped shut, that's all we'll get out of him! Funny, that man draws me and repels me both. He must be hiding something. He looks like Bismarck, don't you think so?

ESTELLE (*bursting out*). A maid! A maid of all work! Antoine left me for a maid! He spent the last years of his life with a maid!

VALÉRIE (*gently*). Don't intoxicate yourself with words, Estelle. That girl was old Frida's niece. That's all we know about her.

CARLOTTA (*roughly*). Anyway what possible difference can it make to you, my dear little Estelle, what the girl was or wasn't? Antoine's dead. She left him and she got married. The play's over. Either way, you can carry on the drama with us – we might pay polite attention to you, even if it drives us all mad, but you can't play your big scene with Antoine now – so?

> *A slight pause. She adds, in a duller tone.*

We're all monsters, we know that. We've made a botched job of it all, we know that too! But we're all on the same train and there's one who gets off at every station. So all we can do now is share out the last sandwiches and comment on the landscape, without thinking too much about the terminus. We owe each other a little bit of mercy, towards the end. We've got to get off each other's backs a bit, dear God. Old loves, old heartaches ... (*Rubbing her knee.*) There's enough to do coping with one's knee.

ESTELLE (*hard*). Speak for yourself, Carlotta. I haven't reached your great age yet. I expect to live a little before then.

CARLOTTA (*in a sudden outburst*). Go on then, live – God save us! – if you've got it in you! It's not what you think it is either, as you'll find out. And it might make you a bit more indulgent. The white gloves of virtue are all very nice but so long as you haven't dipped your hands in the mire like everybody else, you've no right to look down your nose and judge. Live then, go on! You wait, it's no featherbed! Good intentions – we all have those – but you can't do much.

An embarrassed pause follows this tirade. MARCELLIN *repeats absurdly.*

MARCELLIN. Not much. No, not much. (*A pause.*) Anyway, we're here to think about Antoine, who mayn't have been as happy a man as we all thought.

ESTELLE (*shrugging*). Antoine – can't we talk about anybody else? Who *has* been happy, here? Nobody's happy!

MARCELLIN (*going on with his train of thought*). As a medical man, I'm much more sceptical than Lapinet here on the validity of this Herr Freud's new theories. Still, one thing does trouble me. Why should Antoine, on one winter's day, just over three years ago, without a word to anybody, feel the urge to come to the heart of Bavaria to seek out the old nurse he had as a child? Why did he suddenly vanish and never see any one of us again?

ESTELLE (*dryly*). He came back to Paris several times to see his children – in secret.

MARCELLIN. Only his children.

LAPINET. Three years ago – that was the time of *The White Lady* – he'd just had a huge success with it, he was at the height of his fame in Paris, he was lionized, he seemed happy. He saw us then, very often ... Things even seemed to be rather more on the old footing between you, Estelle, weren't they?

MARCELLIN. And then, a sudden decision one afternoon – down the trapdoor and vanish! For good. What on earth could we have done, to give him this imperious need to escape us all?

CARLOTTA (*with a dull growl, as if asleep over her stick in her big armchair*). Don't ferret things out, don't ferret, Marcellin. Life's too short. Keep on nosing about and you'll find what you're looking for and it's always abominable.

A pause. All the characters sit, sunk in thought, except CRAVA-TAR, *who is slowly pacing about upstage. The rhythm of the scene changes, the lighting alters gradually as* MARCELLIN *begins to evoke that evening, three years ago, in Paris.*

MARCELLIN. It's coming back to me now ... The very eve of his departure we had a little supper party, at his house, to celebrate – how like him to think of it too! – the fiftieth performance of his play and his birthday – he was fifty on that day. I can still see you all ... It's strange, we were sitting with him, after supper, or standing about in the drawing-room, chatting, not unlike the way we are here, tonight ... Cravatar was pacing about at the far end of the room. Estelle and Valérie were sitting together, a little apart from the rest, Carlotta was on the sofa. I was finishing a cigar and chatting to Lapinet just as I am now ... The only one missing was Anémone ... No, she wasn't there, at the moment when I'm visualizing the scene. She'd gone out into the garden with her current swain – she'd asked at the last minute if she could bring him along – do you remember, Valérie? You even gave her a comic little telling off on her unladylike behaviour ... And then she came in from the garden with this young man, all rosy from the cold night air ... she

came in during a lull in the talk, a spreading silence, and she said
– I remember it perfectly – 'There's a divine chill in the air!'
Antoine was standing silent behind a great armchair, a half
empty glass in his hand, he seemed not to be seeing us at all . . .
I can call him to mind very well – it's the last image I have of
him . . .

*While he was speaking, the décor, by an effect of lighting, has
blurred. We see a neutral background, where only the furniture
and the people matter.* ANTOINE *mysteriously appearing suddenly through heavy window curtains is half leaning on the high
back of an armchair, just as* MARCELLIN *described him.*
ANÉMONE *enters upstage followed by* ALEXANDER, *both
powdered with snow. The strange scene will be played at first in a
slightly remote way and will then gradually become more real.*

ANÉMONE. There's a divine chill in the air! We've been for a
marvellous walk!

VALÉRIE. Anémone, you'll catch cold if you go on like this.

ANÉMONE. You can't catch cold with Alexis. He's *marvellously*
clever at warming you up.

VALÉRIE. Anémone, apart from your excessive use of the word
marvellous, which I know is in vogue this year, I've asked you a
hundred times to spare us the recital of your fictitious de-
baucheries. I know Alexis, he's far too well behaved to warm
you in any way but with words. Isn't that so, Alexis?

ANÉMONE (*turning to the* YOUNG MAN *who is rather embarrassed*).
Stop blushing, Alexis. You have to say 'Yes, Mamma. I'm very
sorry, Mamma. I shan't do it again, Mamma.' It's a *marvellous*
game parents have invented and the rules are very simple. A
pure young girl of sixteen has never ever been touched by
anybody, never wanted to be touched by anybody and never
will be touched by anybody – until the husband her parents
choose for her will have the right, after a long religious cere-
mony and an interminable and uneatable banquet, to stretch
her naked on a bed and do anything he pleases to her. It's

marvellously simple, isn't it? Antoine, you explained it all to
me, once.

ESTELLE (*annoyed*). I think your daughter is impossible, Valérie!

VALÉRIE (*calm*). My little Anémone, I am a *marvellously* modern
mother, but there are some marvellously modern slaps across
the face too. You richly deserve one. I'm sparing you it out of the
respect due to our host and his guests.

ANÉMONE (*belligerently*). Out of respect for Estelle, whose hand
itches whenever she sets eyes on me? Out of respect for
Antoine? Look at him, he's dying to slap me himself. He's white
with rage. (*She stands squarely in front of him.*) Go on, Antoine!
Hit me! Hit me!

VALÉRIE. Anémone, that's enough! What has Antoine got to do
with any of this?

ANÉMONE. He knows. You don't want to slap my face, Antoine?
Right, I'll do it myself.

> *She slaps herself on both cheeks then turns on her heel and goes
> to the piano upstage where she embarks on an outlandish piece of
> ragtime with one finger.*

VALÉRIE. You should have slapped her, Antoine, as she seems to
think you have the right to. Or at least said something to her.

ANTOINE. I'm fifty years old today. I've no right to say anything
to young girls any more.

VALÉRIE. Not even an insolent little chit – who could be your own
daughter?

ESTELLE (*insidiously*). If Antoine had been her father, Valérie, I
do assure you that Anémone wouldn't have treated him to such
a *marvellously* provocative scene! I should advise you to keep
an eye on them, when he comes to visit. They're the same age,
those two lads, I tell you!

VALÉRIE. That's an absurd thing to say, Estelle!

> *A quivering pause.* MARCELLIN *comes over to them.*

MARCELLIN. You are extraordinary, my old son, you and your

fifty birthdays. Look at me, I'm fifty-one. What is it that bites you so about that number?

ANTOINE. The five.

MARCELLIN. Why, that's flaming youth, dear boy. You're entering into your top form. You're about to give us your real masterpieces.

ANTOINE. You think so? At that age Shakespeare and Molière were at the point of death and Racine had given the whole thing up long ago. I wonder if it isn't a little bumptious of me to persist.

MARCELLIN. Rubbish! In their day they had no hygiene and no medicine, and you're as sound as the Lutine Bell. You're not in the same case as Molière, nor Shakespeare either.

ANTOINE. You said it, not me.

Snatches of laughter at ANTOINE'S *sally with* CRAVATAR'S *grating cackle, from upstage.*

MARCELLIN (*peeved*). There's gloom in your champagne, man, that's all. And sparkle in mine. I drink to your success and your loves.

A quivering silence.

ESTELLE (*clipped*). An angel flew over my grave. There's a whole troop of them about tonight. They must be gathering like birds to fly down to the sun. Marcellin has a gift for the apt word without the gift of leaving it unsaid.

MARCELLIN (*hurt*). Right, I'll keep quiet, then. But as nobody seems to be saying anything at all except me ... Why are you all looking so bootfaced? (*He exclaims absurdly.*) After all, a birthday's a cheerful occasion!

ANTOINE (*absently*). Not mine. Not this year.

VALÉRIE (*laughing*). Because of that five? But you've met it five times already!

ANTOINE. It knew its place then. This year it's putting itself forward.

VALÉRIE (*still laughing*). And I haven't even got you a present. What would you like for your birthday, Antoine?

ANTOINE (*gloomily*). One year less.

> *He rises and goes upstage in silence to watch* ANÉMONE *who is softly playing the piano.*

ESTELLE (*with a bitter little laugh to the others*). It's an obsession! He's been ill with it ever since this morning. And the odd thing is, yesterday it didn't even cross his mind. The children were very funny. They went into his room and woke him with a big white cottonwool beard they'd made, a crooked stick and fifty boxes of cough sweets.

MARCELLIN. Did he laugh?

ESTELLE. Yes, madly. He put on the beard and he hobbled about and coughed and sucked his sweets until lunchtime in his pyjamas, acting the dotard for them. They ended up having a pillow fight, deluging the room with feathers and soaking one another with the bathspray. So the housekeeper gave notice. That was *my* birthday present. *When* is he going to grow up?

CRAVATAR. You are funny, Estelle!

ESTELLE (*a little nettled*). Oh, always. That's all that's left to me, being funny. Because Antoine never makes things very funny, I can tell you.

CRAVATAR (*perfidiously*). You do surprise me! Writing about his *White Lady* – which I'll admit I didn't care for much – some of my fellow critics went so far as to call him our modern Molière.

ESTELLE. I'm sorry for Molière's wife then. It couldn't have been fun every day at home.

CRAVATAR (*insidiously*). No. But she paid him out for it, remember. Which gave us two masterpieces as a result. (*He adds.*) You might try it yourself, if only for Antoine's career. You never know.

LAPINET (*very much the academic*). You know, recognized authorities on Molière have exploded the myth of the link between his private life and his work. I'm always flooring my students by

pointing out that his most misogynistic play was written directly
after his marriage, during a period of great happiness.

ANTOINE (*who has come back and heard this*). What professors,
who know everything, will never know, Lapinet, for all their
sleepless nights, are the secrets of creativeness. Molière and I
share the same trade – you'll forgive invidious comparisons –
and I can tell you this. You always write about what's going to
happen and after that you live it. In the fragile bliss of his honeymoon, Molière lived through his wife's first betrayal.

LAPINET (*a little peeved*). It's all quite simple then. Tell us the
plot of your next play and we'll know what's going to happen.

ANTOINE. I hit on the theme this morning, as I woke up half a
century old. A man has just died – not having lived any too
commendably – not given very much, and not received very
much either – having, in short, perhaps through his own fault,
let friendship pass him by, and love. The day of the funeral, all
the people in his life meet for the traditional meal together in his
house – a country custom, but let's say he died in the country.
And they draw up a balance sheet, on him and on themselves.
That's all. But it will be quite funny.

CRAVATAR. Just that – no action?

ANTOINE. No, obviously. The action died out before the curtain
goes up.

CARLOTTA (*grunting*). Very dismal that's going to be, dear boy.
You've got to keep things moving in the theatre. No. No. You
must give us a heroic piece, with huge emotions, something in
the great tradition. Look at *Hamlet*. Every time a hit. Except
when they let that old monster Sarah tear it to shreds with a peg
leg.

CRAVATAR. So, if I follow you, it's a kind of Russian effort is it,
like the things they're trying to fob us off with these days? You
believe in all this mood drama, do you? Paris audiences are used
to a brisk tempo, they don't like it when it drags. And as for this
new-fangled idea of making plays out of everyday trivia —

ANTOINE. Don't write your notice, Cravatar, the play's not

written yet. There might be a few funny bits and one or two theatrical devices – put in for their own sake – I adore them, it's a weakness of mine.

MARCELLIN. What are you going to call it?

ANTOINE. *Dear Antoine,* or *The Love That Failed.*

CARLOTTA (*grunting*). Rotten title.

Another quivering pause.

ESTELLE (*quietly*). Another angel. We ought to have a rifle. I'd like to shoot one down, just once. Just to see what the little creatures look like.

CRAVATAR (*hard*). No need for that, Estelle. You're an angel yourself. An angel with too much patience.

ANTOINE (*going to him, with sudden roughness*). May one ask what you mean by that, Cravatar?

CRAVATAR (*equally brutally*). I mean that you behave foully to Estelle! And it gets on all our nerves, at times.

A fairly long, tense pause. One wonders if the two men are about to come to blows. Then ANTOINE breaks the tension.

ANTOINE (*lightly*). I'm sure you're right. I'm irritable, pointlessly bitter – and something of a cad. And my jokes are always the kind you hear in public baths. But there, what can I do? Since this morning, I'm learning to be old.

He turns upstage where ANÉMONE is still at the piano, gazing into space and playing softly. ESTELLE has risen and started to pour the coffee which a servant has silently brought in. A vague hum of words. 'Sugar? Please. Two. Only half a cup, or I shan't sleep. How do you get your cook to make such good coffee? None to be had anywhere in Paris now.' But they are dreamlike words, stifled, furtive. One must only be aware of ANTOINE and ANÉMONE at the far end of the room. ANÉMONE has stopped playing. She looks at him and says.

ANÉMONE. I'm an idiot, aren't I?

ANTOINE (*gently*). No. You're what one always dreams of finding. You are the illusion of love. But you're sixteen. It's as if I fell in love with the shape of a cloud, on the seashore, in a high wind.

> ANÉMONE *says nothing and starts to play again softly. The set appears gradually in a different light. We are in Bavaria again.* ANTOINE, *who can remain where he is, glass in hand, elbow on the piano, stands as if eclipsed. When the lighting is back to normal,* MARCELLIN *is finishing his story.*

MARCELLIN. And we went on chatting of this and that until the time came to leave. He said nothing, just listened at the back, glass in hand, as if he'd already left us. I have the feeling that he'd asked us a question that night, a question not one of us was able to answer.

> *A pause.* CARLOTTA *growls.*

CARLOTTA. What question?

MARCELLIN. Perhaps the question that Mozart, who never grew up either, used, it seems, to ask everyone he met . . . Do you love me?

> *A frozen silence. Only* CRAVATAR *paces about upstage. The dog starts to howl. The curtain slowly falls.*

Act Three

FRIDA *shows in the characters, laden with rugs and suitcases, wearing somewhat showy travelling clothes. They are hot. It is summer. The characters are the same people, and yet it will take a little while to understand quite why they are different.* FRIDA *says something to them in German and goes out.*

ACTRESS CARLOTTA. What did she say?

ACTOR MARCELLIN. She's going to tell him we've arrived.

ACTOR LAPINET (*taking possession of the room like the leading man treading the stage*). Believe me or believe me not, it's infernally hot. Bavaria in summer-time is the White Man's Grave. Anybody else but him and nothing would have dragged me here. A bit part six hundred miles from Paris for someone of my standing – I don't care what you say, it's hardly in my line.

ACTRESS CARLOTTA. No, but the pay's good.

ACTOR LAPINET (*with a shrug*). Never good enough!

ACTRESS CARLOTTA. And he might bring the play into Paris!

ACTOR LAPINET. This one? I'd take a bet on it! Did you read it on the train? Darling, it's dementia! I really can't think what possessed him to write something as insipid as that. Where's the man who wrote *The White Lady*? I can see why he's not put pen to paper all this time. He's written out. That's why.

ACTRESS CARLOTTA. It's got atmosphere.

ACTOR LAPINET (*chanting*). Atmosphere – atmosphere! We'll cover ourselves with scorn and derision, darling, that's about all. Thank God the press won't be there. He said in his letter it was to be privately performed. That's the only reason I agreed to do it. (*To the* ACTOR CRAVATAR.) What part have you got, old love?

ACTOR CRAVATAR. The Doctor.

ACTOR LAPINET. Ah yes. The feckless friend. Nice little role. Two or three sure laughs. Vintage St Flour.

ACTOR CRAVATAR (*ironically*). Almost Molière.

ACTOR LAPINET (*ditto*). Oh, quite. Well, let's say bad Congreve. But effective. (*To the* ACTOR MARCELLIN.) What's he given you, Gramont?

ACTOR MARCELLIN. The critic.

ACTOR LAPINET (*a little surprised*). Fancy. I see you more as the Doctor myself. Subtle part that.

ACTOR MARCELLIN (*wryly*). A cameo, yes. Terribly under-written. He should have carried him through to the end.

ACTOR LAPINET. Have a heart! His patient commits suicide!

ACTRESS ANÉMONE. I don't understand that ingenue of his one bit! Pure as the driven snow and twice as virginal!

ACTOR LAPINET (*paternally*). Don't be scared of it, my sweet. You're an actress, you should be able to convey that.

ACTRESS ANÉMONE (*nettled*). I have played virgins before, thank you. But why does he give her all those filthy things to say?

ACTOR LAPINET. It's the new wave. Look at Bernstein and his ilk. Brutalism is the trend just now. Audacity is all very fine, but where will it lead the theatre, answer me that? Of course they've got their cronies to whip it all up to a froth in the weeklies but it doesn't catch on with the Great French Public. Up Cyrano! That's theatre! I must say I'm staggered to see an old pro like St Flour drop into the same bucket. What has he sunk to?

ACTOR MARCELLIN. It's a private performance. A drawing-room piece, literally. He's having fun, that's all.

ACTOR LAPINET (*sighing*). Let's hope the audience will. It makes no odds to me, I sell my pound of ham, but what with the expense of it, he'll be paying through the nose for his little bit of fun.

ACTRESS CARLOTTA. Private performance in the stately home, very blue-blooded, you must admit. Antoine has always been a

E

prince at heart. Do you remember the hundredth performance of *The Snare* in the gardens of the Ritz? What a triumph!

ACTOR LAPINET. Pooh. The hundredth, with money flowing like water – that's the easiest thing to bring off in the theatre. It's the first that takes the doing!

He notices a small, makeshift stage at the end of the big hall.

Don't tell me that's the stage! It's going to be infernally cramped, this production.

He goes to ACTRESS GABRIELLE *who is sitting knitting in a corner with* ACTRESS VALÉRIE.

ACTRESS GABRIELLE. Cable stitch is three plain two purl, and then you twist it, you see, which is the tricky bit.

VALÉRIE. You'll have to write it down for me. I'll give you my recipe for mushroom tart.

ACTOR LAPINET. Not at it already, you two, with your knitting and your recipes? What is the profession coming to! In my young day the men wanted a fancy piece on every touring date, and the women looked out for a rich fool to pay their hotel bill! Ah, I was born two centuries too late! (*He adds.*) Of course, I wouldn't have got the Legion of Honour then.

ACTRESS GABRIELLE. Look, my old lad, if you didn't knit in the theatre you'd really be wasting your time, there are so many waits.

ACTOR LAPINET. Talking of waits, you'd be better employed learning your lines, my pearl. Remember what happened in *L'Arlésienne* last year, you dried on me in my big scene.

ACTRESS GABRIELLE. I know this backwards.

ACTOR LAPINET (*with a sigh*). You're lucky. I think it's all so inane I can't get it into my head. Oh well, I've played in asinine fatuities before.

ANTOINE *has just entered in a handsome floral dressing-gown which gives him the air of a Samurai.* LAPINET *rushes over to him, transformed.*

Ah, Maestro! Dear Maestro! What a joy it is to see you again!

ANTOINE. Delighted to see you too, Grossac. The management weren't too difficult about your taking time off?

ACTOR LAPINET. For you, Maestro, one can ask the earth, even at the Comédie Française! Don't forget, they're still hoping for a play from you!

ANTOINE (*shaking hands all round*). Delighted to see you, all of you. You smell divinely of Paris.

ACTRESS CARLOTTA. We left there last night ...

ANTOINE. I can breathe it all round you. (*He gathers them affectionately to him and cries.*) Ah, it's good to be backstage again, surrounded by actors. Believe me that's the only place where anything happens. When you venture outside it's a wilderness – and chaos. Life is unreal, I can tell you that. First of all it has no shape. Nobody knows the lines and they always miss their cue. One should never set foot outside a theatre. It's the only place on earth where the human adventure is fit for consumption. (*He clasps them to him looking at them all affectionately.*) I do hope we're all going to enjoy ourselves. Do you know your lines?

There is a half-hearted murmur. He laughs.

No, of course you don't. And a good thing too. You know I can't stand that. Learn as you rehearse, that's the only way.

ACTOR CRAVATAR (*sourly*). I know mine, the part's so short.

ANTOINE (*smiling*). Yes, but it's a doctor! And doctors and clergymen – I needn't tell an old fox like you that! – always steal the show.

ACTOR CRAVATAR. It helps if they open their mouths.

ANTOINE. Now, don't be bitter. I'll give you a few more lines in Act One. (*To* ACTOR MARCELLIN.) What do you think of the critic, do you like the part?

ACTOR MARCELLIN. Interesting. But it's rather daring.

ANTOINE. We have to dare a bit too. They're daring enough in their reviews.

ACTOR MARCELLIN. You don't think it's going a little far to name the actual paper?

ANTOINE. Don't worry, the real fellow won't be in the audience. Our little barbs are just for us. You'll see, the play itself's a trifle, an excuse, and faintly baroque in mood. It was the characters I found amusing. And I think I've cast them rather well. (*He looks at them all, amused and murmurs.*) Uncannily so, though I say it myself. The more one has to do with the theatre, the more one sees that casting is the beginning and the end of it. The main thing is to choose actors with the aura of the part.

ACTRESS CARLOTTA (*simpering*). Have I got the right aura? I know one can do a lot with make up, but you've cast me as an old crone, maestro!

ANTOINE (*kindly*). Come, come. A great tragedienne with a touch of the picturesque, that's all.

ACTRESS CARLOTTA. They say in the script she's a hundred!

ANTOINE (*smiling*). They're exaggerating a bit.

ACTRESS CARLOTTA. She's cynical! She's foul!

ANTOINE. She's real! She aims low, so she aims true. Shall I tell you something? Behind all her outrageousness, *she's* the one with sense. In point of fact – if you want the basic source of it – the old tragedienne is me!

ACTOR LAPINET (*importantly*). Tell me then, maestro, if it's not indiscreet, is your play autobiographical to some extent?

ANTOINE (*with a snort of laughter*). What nonsense! I'm not dead, am I?

ACTOR LAPINET. Yes, but the title. *Dear Antoine* or *The Love That Failed.*

ANTOINE. Just a title, dear fellow! It's all purely imaginary.

ACTRESS ESTELLE (*stepping forward*). But what is Geneviève, exactly? I can't get her character very clearly in the lines.

ANTOINE. I'll tell you. Geneviève is an unfulfilled woman. That's the key to the whole character.

ACTRESS ESTELLE. Did she ever love Antoine?

ANTOINE. Indeed she did.

ACTRESS ESTELLE. She ought to grieve for him then. You've given her some dreadful things to say.

ANTOINE. She does grieve for him, and she says some dreadful things – which isn't absolutely contradictory.

ACTRESS ESTELLE. When Antoine was unfaithful to her, was she hurt?

ANTOINE. I'm sure she was. But it takes a very good chemist to analyse the pain of love. And one can seldom do it for oneself. It's other people, with keener eyes, who can see the traces of spleen or the black residue of pride at the bottom of a test-tubeful of tears.

ACTRESS CARLOTTA. So you don't believe in tears, then, maestro?

ANTOINE. Not a lot, no. Nor in the purity of heartbreak either. Whatever the horrors of the situation, one always weeps a little for oneself. As a matter of fact, I'd thought at one point of calling my play 'Thank you, my widow is alive and well'.

ACTRESS CARLOTTA (*exclaiming roguishly*). You're wicked, maestro! If you believe all that, you must be the unhappiest man on earth!

ANTOINE (*lightly*). I am, quite the unhappiest. But I'm also the one who takes his unhappiness best. Heaven sent me the gift of making others laugh at it.

FRIDA *and a kind of little peasant* VALET *have come in and start to pick up the luggage.* ANTOINE *goes on without a pause.*

Ah, Frida will show you to your rooms. They're a little rustic you'll find, but cool and very pleasant. My old Frida, who brought me up, hasn't spoken French for forty years, and the boy doesn't either. You'll have to use sign language. There used to be a girl here, who kept house for me and she spoke French beautifully, but she went away unfortunately and we'll have to muddle through without her. All I ask is that you unpack, change if you want – and come straight down again.

Despite the fatigues of travelling we can't afford the luxury of a wasted morning. I mean to open in a week.

ACTOR LAPINET (*exclaiming*). But we'll never do it!

ANTOINE. The play's so short! In the theatre one always says one will never do it and one always does. At five to eight the scenery collapses, the juvenile lead, who's expecting a baby, faints in the wings, the star has left her teeth up in her dressing-room, the curtain goes up and at the end it's Austerlitz!

ACTOR LAPINET (*gloomily*). Or Waterloo.

ANTOINE. You forget, my dear fellow, Waterloo was also a great victory. Wellington was desperate. At six o'clock the battle was lost. Along came Blucher. Saved!

ACTOR LAPINET (*under his breath to* CARLOTTA, *as they go out*). He's become very pro-German! If he goes on like this, I shall throw a temperament!

ACTRESS CARLOTTA. I've heard it said he's living with a Bavarian girl who's young enough to be his daughter. You know, at that age, love can drive a man to anything.

> *They have gone out.* ANTOINE *moves to the* GIRL *who is playing the part of Maria, takes her arm as she is about to go out and says simply.*

ANTOINE. Mademoiselle, you're the only one I haven't met before. I cast you from a photograph because you looked so very like the part. But I'm told you're very talented too. Yours is almost a non-speaking role. It may seem insignificant, but it's the kingpin of the play. I'll explain it presently. There, among all those talkative women who analyse themselves, you, Mademoiselle, are Love, the true kind, the love that gives and hardly says a word.

ACTRESS MARIA. All the other characters think she's silly and rather hard . . .

ANTOINE (*gently*). That's an immense privilege reserved for the pure in heart. She isn't hard – she's clear cut. She isn't brainless, she's tender. She alone, probably, feels any real pain and that's why she doesn't speak. She has nothing much save one scene at the end – but believe me, I'm a good judge – it's the best part in the play.

ACTRESS MARIA. I don't understand her very well. She comes back for the funeral, yet she'd left Antoine some time before to get married?

ANTOINE. Yes.

ACTRESS MARIA. Didn't she love him any more? It isn't very clearly stated in the play.

ANTOINE. Yes. She loved him.

ACTRESS MARIA. And did he?

ANTOINE. Yes, he loved her too.

ACTRESS MARIA. Then why did they part?

ANTOINE. That's one of the dark areas in my play. I'd like people to wonder why. I wonder why myself, dammit!

ACTRESS MARIA. I do think, if I'm to play the part properly, that I really ought to know why she decided – or agreed – to leave him.

ANTOINE (*lightly*). Oh, these actors who always must know everything! And Paris is nothing to Germany! You can't get them to lift their little finger without a whole analysis in depth! (*He turns grave again and says tonelessly.*) Possibly she realized that Antoine had never been capable of living – that he'd invented his life and the characters in it, at the same time as he wrote his plays and in the same way – and that she was just a symbol, like the others, in a slumbering man's dream. That day, she fled, like a little wild animal who smells the wind of death.

There is a pause. The GIRL'*s eyes suddenly fill with tears. She murmurs.*

ACTRESS MARIA. And he let her go?

ANTOINE (*softly*). He even helped her to, a little, without knowing what he was doing, quite. There are some human beings who are possessed by solitude and who don't know how to hold on to others. And then again, people always talk about age differences. Faces are nothing. It's the souls that wear the wrinkles. So one day, she came to him and said —

ACTRESS MARIA (*softly, mysteriously*). I need to live . . .

He looks at her, suddenly disturbed. She goes on smiling.

I have to build a house for myself too. The only house *I* shall ever have. Without you . . .

She has said this quietly, sadly, with an imperceptible smile which makes one wonder whether she is acting or not. ANTOINE *murmurs, as if fascinated.*

ANTOINE. Why, you know your lines already?

The GIRL *goes on softly, her eyes fixed on him, as they stand face to face, disturbingly aware of each other.*

ACTRESS MARIA. Because some things are real – and they aren't necessarily the funny things . . . You'll come to see that one day, when you finally grow up and you stop wanting to play. But it will be rather late.

ANTOINE (*fascinated, murmurs, faraway*). And he says . . . Yes, it is getting late.

ACTRESS MARIA (*with a ghost of a movement*). I'll light the lamps . . .

ANTOINE (*quietly*). No, I didn't mean that.

They stand face to face, very still. He goes on, in a neutral tone, almost lightly, smiling a little as if it were a game.

If you tell me that you've decided to leave, I shan't do anything to stop you, you know that, don't you? At my age, one's crammed with inhibitions – and I really can't throw myself at your feet. The heart is willing, but the knees won't do it. A foretaste of rheumatism perhaps. Ageing men don't go down on their knees, because they can't be absolutely sure of getting up again.

ACTRESS MARIA (*smiling a strange smile*). I know you won't kneel at my feet – I know you'll go on smiling right until the end, as if you didn't mind. But I do know you loved me – in your fashion.

ANTOINE. Yes. And you still mean to marry that lad, whom you don't love?

ACTRESS MARIA. He's strong – he's uncomplicated. I was promised to him before I met you and I know he's waited for me. He'll surround me with real things – a little lustreless, but real. And those are what I need now.

ANTOINE (*murmuring*). Real things – what are they?

ACTRESS MARIA (*with a grave smile*). Children, homes . . . He'll give me a real child and I'll look after a real home – the life that was mapped out for me as a little German country girl – which you disrupted for a moment. Cutting real bread and butter at four o'clock for my boy when I hear him running back from school in his galoshes over the hard snow outside.

ANTOINE (*dully*). And will you be happy?

ACTRESS MARIA. I shan't stop loving you, I don't suppose, and he will know it. But I told you he was rough hewn and uncomplicated. He'll accept me as I am, I know. In return I'll give him my strength and my faith, to travel the road beside him.

ANTOINE (*light and steely again*). And when you've finished cutting all that bread and butter and your brat's asleep, you'll give yourself to him, won't you, at night, in your God awful German bed without sheets?

ACTRESS MARIA (*harder suddenly*). Yes. (*She adds succinctly.*) Lovingly. Because that will be his due, and I don't cheat. And because he's handsome and young and strong and because I'll be his wife.

ANTOINE. And you'll forget me?

ACTRESS MARIA (*clearly*). No. I'll put you back in your rightful place, along with Paris, where I never went but once – with you, one whirlwind of a day; along with the theatre once a year in Munich, at the Opera House, for the Congress of Bavarian Teachers. Along with France, where everything is lighter,

easier, kindlier than it is at home with us – but which isn't home
. . . You know it well enough, you knew it as a small child – I
belong to a breed where you eat up your dry bread without
complaining . . .

There is an anguishing pause and then ANTOINE *suddenly
breaks the spell and cries in a different tone of voice.*

ANTOINE. Etcetera – etcetera . . . ! Pretty little scene, that, I must
say. A bit wordy and high flown, a little sentimental too, perhaps. But have you noticed? – it's the cynics who weep the easy
tears!

ACTRESS MARIA (*on the verge of tears, murmurs*). I think it's so
terribly sad . . .

ANTOINE (*with a whoop, as he seizes her in his arms*). My poor little
sparrow! Who the devil lumbered me with an actress like you?
If you start believing in theatrical make-believe you'll die before
your time, my child.

ACTRESS MARIA (*startled*). What are you doing?

ANTOINE. Kissing you. Because I feel like it!

Old FRIDA, *who has come back in for the* GIRL'*s suitcase,
catches them kissing and cries venemously.*

FRIDA. Französer! Gauner!

ANTOINE (*yelling at her, still holding the* GIRL). Yes! I'm kissing
this one as well! Yes! I'll stoop to anything and I'll die like a
dog! But couldn't you say it in French, you old Walkyrie? You
know I couldn't ever learn your German gibberish.

*The others have come in at the same moment, catching them at it
too. In the group* CARLOTTA *is heard muttering* 'Of course, with
Antoine, the ingénue always goes through the mill . . .'
ANTOINE *goes to them, lightly, very naturally.*

Ah there you are! We'll walk through the opening scene . . .
This is a play that has to be attacked sixteen to the bar in a
high key. Later, with the andante, the mood changes. Let's go!
Places for Act One! Have you all got your scripts?

He has clambered up on to the rostrum, as happy as a child at play.

On stage, everyone, tiny though it is! Off the boards there's no salvation! An actor is first and foremost someone who's climbed on to something – be it only a soapbox. Ask any politician – they know about play-acting – give them one word to say at a meeting and hup! On to their perches! The French Revolution started with Camille Desmoulins up on a chair!

He paces about the little stage, setting chairs.

This is just a makeshift arrangement. We'll modify it as the need arises. Anyway, the whole of the beginning is played standing up. The Doctor friend and Geneviève come on first. They're looking over this completely unknown house, to which the Lawyer has summoned them on Antoine's death. The others are still in the next room. They come in later. Do you get the feel of it? Antoine didn't only betray Geneviève with a woman, he betrayed her with a house. In the theatre, the situation is all. It's taken me thirty years to see it. Off we go!

The ACTRESS ESTELLE *and the* ACTOR CRAVATAR *begin reading from their scripts, rather badly, it must be said.* ANTOINE *has settled himself on a chair, below them and a little apart from the others. With complete naturalness he puts his arm round the* ACTRESS MARIA'S *shoulders.*

ACTOR CRAVATAR (*miming his entrance with the* ACTRESS ESTELLE *on to the little stage*). A little gem of baroque decoration in a sixteenth-century setting. It's splendid.

ACTRESS ESTELLE (*reading*). Yes, Antoine always did have splendid houses. It was a disease with him. Whenever he liked a place, he had to buy a house there. He'd convinced himself – just because we'd spent the happiest part of our honeymoon there – that Florence should be the scene of our reconciliation. Any other man would have taken a suite at the Grand Hotel, he bought a villa at Fiesole, where we only spent one day. Just time for a quarrel – a final one as it turned out. (*She breaks off and says to* ANTOINE.) Does she put any bitterness into that?

ANTOINE. No. Detached. She's stating a fact. What should come over is a certain air of aridity and lack of warmth – in contrast with her widow's weeds. All in brisk tempo as I said – very lively.

ACTRESS ESTELLE (*going on*). Later on, when we decided – mutually – to send Philippe away to school, the very thought of seeing the boy on Sundays in a restaurant made him quite ill. So he bought a house two miles away. Four walls and a roof were his way of believing in the family. He never asked himself what was to be put inside.

ANTOINE. A chord. Point it.

ACTRESS ESTELLE (*going on*). Faced with the problem of his monthly visit to the children (he refused to come back home to the Avenue Foch – although I was more than glad to receive him) you'd think he'd have taken a room at the Ritz. Not Antoine. For this new piece of family adultery, he bought and furnished a two-roomed bachelor flat in Montmartre, where the concierge, who knew the local morals, made I don't know how many reports to the police to say that her new tenant was corrupting boys and girls of tender age – Marie-Christine and Philippe went there you see, by turns, to spend the night. Grandchâtre, the Préfêt —

ANTOINE. Did I put Grandchâtre?

ACTRESS ESTELLE. Yes.

ANTOINE. He'll think he's being got at. You'd better make it Petitchâtre. The merest detail will reassure a fool.

ACTRESS ESTELLE (*altering her script with her pencil*). Petitchâtre even sent for him, very concerned, and urged him to be a little more discreet in his vices.

ACTOR CRAVATAR (*lugubriously*). How wildly funny.

ANTOINE. One would never guess.

ACTOR CRAVATAR (*dazed*). What?

ANTOINE. – That it's wildly funny. You said that like a dirge. It amuses you, man!

ACTOR CRAVATAR (*sourly*). The trouble is it doesn't much.

ANTOINE. I'm sorry about that, but that would entail a basic re-assessment of what acting's all about. Be so kind, would you, as to act as if it did amuse you.

ACTOR CRAVATAR (*slapping his sides*). How wildly funny.

A short pause. ANTOINE *gives a sigh.*

ACTRESS ESTELLE (*continuing*). Wasn't it? I schooled myself, with Antoine, always to treat everything as wildly funny. I spent fifteen years flaunting screams of laughter and floods of tears.

ACTOR CRAVATAR (*overdoing it again*). Poor Geneviève!

A very slight pause. ANTOINE *sighs again.*

ACTRESS ESTELLE (*echoing him*). Poor Geneviève. That's what everyone in Paris said. I used to be just Geneviève. I won myself a second name. Poor-Geneviève. With a hyphen. Poor! Winning little name. One that suits me so well. Don't you think so?

ACTOR CRAVATAR (*again doing far too much and practically squeezing up to her*). You're maligning yourself. I know lots of men, myself included, who —

ANTOINE (*shouting irritably*). You don't have to do that much! He's not going to tumble her in the drawing-room!

ACTOR CRAVATAR (*tersely*). Does he or does he not want her?

ANTOINE. Geneviève is ravishing and he'd be only too delighted if the chance were offered. But that doesn't make him a cave-man panting after his first female of the day. He's not slavering at the mouth. Keep it light.

ACTOR CRAVATAR (*sourly*). Oh, quite, one can't do a single thing of one's own, one never can.

ANTOINE. That's often the best plan in the theatre. Two times out of three the lines are enough.

ACTOR CRAVATAR (*ironically*). And the third?

Stifled giggles from the actors at this.

ANTOINE (*impassively*). Let's get on.

ACTRESS ESTELLE. Spare me that old song. I'd decided, in our lopsided relationship, that one of us at least would remain faithful – to even things up a little.

ACTOR CRAVATAR. Faithful to whom? To what?

ACTRESS ESTELLE (*briefly*). To myself, let's say.

ANTOINE. Yes, that you did very well. It's one of the keys to the character. People always have a soft spot for faithful women, but as somebody once said, I can't think who now – there is a kind of fidelity which is only to oneself.

ACTRESS CARLOTTA (*from her seat*). You're wicked, maestro! You destroy everything.

ANTOINE (*with an airy wave of the hand*). Oh, just words, you know – just words. You play the cynic, you think you're being very clever, you raise a little laughter; you destroy nothing. Even with genius you don't. Do you think, after Tartuffe's unmasking that hypocrites felt one whit less complacent? Man's a sturdy monster. (*He carries straight on.*) I'd like to cut for the moment to the entrance of the other characters. Let's see if you'll all fit on to my little stage. We'll rehearse straight through this afternoon. Grossac, Grandmont, our diva, Chanteraine, the girl – on stage and let me set your entrances.

The others go up on to the rostrum, ANTOINE *gives them their positions for* CARLOTTA's *entrance then steps down again.*

Off you go. It's only roughed out, but I think it's quite good.

ACTRESS CARLOTTA (*before starting her lines*). She's a crazy old witch – shouldn't I characterize?

ANTOINE (*impassively*). I don't think that will be necessary, my sweet.

ACTRESS CARLOTTA (*simpering*). Even so, I'm not quite the right age for the part.

The others snigger under their breaths at this remark.

ANTOINE (*still impassively*). We can do it with lighting. Carry on.

ACTRESS CARLOTTA (*launching into her part*). Admirable road! Fabulous precipices! Delicious sensation of danger! House and setting both extraordinary! All of it perfection! (*She kisses* VALÉRIE *theatrically*.) Another kiss, cara mia.

ACTRESS ESTELLE (*sotto voce to* MARCELLIN). She always sounds like a telegram.

ACTRESS CARLOTTA. Does she know she's got the wrong widow?

ANTOINE. Clearly.

ACTRESS CARLOTTA. Then I'll have to point it up. Another kiss, cara mia!

She overdoes the gestures.

ANTOINE (*patiently*). Not quite so much, perhaps, or it won't be funny.

ACTRESS CARLOTTA. Forgive me, my dear maestro, but you must make up your mind what you want.

ANTOINE (*patiently*). I have. Something between the two, as always. Let's go on, we'll do the fine points later.

ACTRESS CARLOTTA. Another kiss, cara mia!

ACTRESS ESTELLE. She always sounds like a telegram.

ACTRESS CARLOTTA (*pretending to discover her mistake*). Oh what a dizzy silly I am! Both of them in black, both so sad, I thought it was Estelle! I'm so sorry, dear girl. (*She goes to* ESTELLE.) It was you I meant to kiss, cara mia! (*She clasps her vigorously to her vast bosom.*) Without resentment and with all my heart. Oh, the immense, immense grief of it. Let us sit down. (*She goes to a chair.*) Beautiful stage chair. He always did have a flair for unearthing a piece nobody had ever seen before. The unbending grandeur of the seventeenth century with a rather Germanic excess of gilt. (*She asks.*) Will it be this chair?

ANTOINE (*irritably*). No, of course not. Go on.

ACTRESS CARLOTTA. 'Unsittable on.' (*Grouchily.*) So it is too. Unsittable on! A kitchen chair, I ask you! Absurd not rehearsing with the proper furniture.

ANTOINE. Carry on.

ACTRESS CARLOTTA. We aren't machines, dear maestro, we're sensitive human beings . . . (*She goes on, stressing the line.*) Unsittable on. I shall try the sofa. (*She looks round for it and asks archly.*) Will there be a sofa?

ANTOINE (*worried*). I'm wondering that myself. If I bring a sofa on, there'll be no room to move.

ACTRESS CARLOTTA (*irked*). If there isn't a sofa, we'll have to cut my line and I don't want to lose it. It's my first laugh.

ACTOR LAPINET (*stepping forward, nobly*). May I give you my opinion, dear maestro? This whole thing is sheer improvisation. We'll never open in a week, it's impossible.

ANTOINE. Nothing's impossible in the theatre, as you well know.

ACTOR LAPINET (*with mounting temper*). The way we're going on I can safely predict an evening of amateur dramatics, my dear fellow.

ANTOINE. I do hope, my dear Grossac, that we still are amateurs and will remain so, always. It's the most decried term in the theatre and the only one with the word love at the root of it – if you know your Latin. Anyway, in the theatre, we're always learners, thank God. Very depressing it would be if we stopped being surprised.

ACTOR LAPINET. Pardon me, maestro, but I do have thirty-five years at the Comédie Française behind me!

ANTOINE (*smiling*). I do see that could be a handicap.

ACTOR LAPINET (*swathing himself in his dignity*). If you're going to take that attitude!

ANTOINE. My dear Grossac, I was joking. Nobody could have greater respect for your illustrious house than I. I respect it so much that I haven't yet dared to enter the repertoire.

ACTOR LAPINET (*exploding*). But God dammit all! If you want to do any old thing, any old how, why ask experienced professionals to do it? And before whom were you intending to perform this load of rubbish anyway?

ANTOINE (*cryptically*). Only myself.

The others, surprised by the unexpectedness of his reply have stopped the indignant mutterings which underlined the old actor's rebelliousness. They look at ANTOINE.

It was one last, rather bitter pleasure I wanted to indulge in. To summon the characters of my life and for once, to write the script – the real one – the script that's never talked about. For once to do the staging of it. To be able to stop you when you weren't doing it right, to turn your backs to the audience at the most pregnant moment and see if your rumps could act as well. To stop your mouths . . . to send you back to your non-existent nothing if need be, when you were too bad. All the things one never does with the real people in one's life.

ACTOR LAPINET (*indignantly*). But good God Almighty, sir! The theatre is a sacred art. It's not a toy! Am I to understand that we were just guinea pigs in a sort of experiment in vivisection?

ANTOINE (*with a strange smile*). A bit, yes.

ACTOR LAPINET. It's beyond belief! Sir, in forty years in the profession I have never seen the like of it! So we were going to memorize the text, were we? – and perform it before you for your own private gratification?

ANTOINE. One never writes for anything else but one's own private gratification.

ACTOR LAPINET. But that's an orgy for Nero!

ANTOINE. What a big word! I had a little fun imagining what you would say over my coffin, I think I'm entitled to that. Only I made one basic error. I see now why I wasn't getting the enjoyment I'd hoped for out of this rehearsal. It wasn't *you* talking, it was you *seen by me*. There's no escaping that. It's a cage. We can only know others through the idea we form of them ourselves. Other people – what an incomprehensible world! The true pleasure – the one so many men must have dreamed of – would be to lie there – good and stiff in the box, but not quite

F

dead – and to listen, for the very first time, to those strangers one lived one's life among.

He looks around him with a sort of sardonic gleam. Then he asks abruptly.

What will you say, exactly, on that day? What do people say? As senior member of the Comédie Française, you must be used to funerals?

ACTOR LAPINET (*misconstruing him*). Well now . . . subduing our heartfelt grief, we would speak of the immense loss to our profession . . . We would call to mind the courteous, charming man – the tireless worker . . . We'd reminisce on the long hours of rewarding toil together, during weeks of gruelling rehearsals —

ANTOINE (*roaring with laughter*). No, no! Not you! Your characters! The characters I asked you to impersonate. They're the ones I'd like to hear! The over-frivolous friend, the over-ponderous one, the false-hearted soul-mate, the widow. (*With a light flourish he gives* ACTRESS ESTELLE'S *hand a comic little kiss.*) My widow! To think you wander through a lifetime beside your embryonic widow and you don't even know who she is. And at the sudden birth of that enigmatic little person – phwtt! It's too late to get to know her – you're dead! (*He exclaims strangely.*) Oh, my lady, I should so like to have known you. (*He carries straight on, in a sudden fever of inspiration.*) Listen, friends! You studied the characters you're playing in the train, and by some coincidence – not totally unaccountable to me, I'll admit – you make them disturbingly real. Suppose you tried to play it – that scene, I mean, I should enjoy it so!

ACTOR LAPINET (*appalled*). Are you asking us to improvise?

ANTOINE. Why not? I'm told it's all the rage these days. Go on, play me the scene I couldn't write – for the simple reason that I couldn't run to the luxury of a change of set. Play me the cemetery scene. It's a gift. The plot's simple. You've all come to Bavaria at my lawyer's request – it's a rare thing not to respond to a summons of that sort. You've toiled up to the little grave-yard on the mountain-side. And there you all are, in the little baroque chapel, around the tomb. There's a brief moment of embarrassment, you don't know quite what to say ... And then, finally, somebody plucks up courage and says something ... preferably something really trite ...

He sets some chairs and lies down on them, with an expression of huge enjoyment.

There we are. I'm playing the corpse.

He shouts at them as they stand looking at him hesitantly.

Get on with it, damn you!

ACTOR LAPINET. You're asking us to do something very tricky indeed, dear maestro.

ANTOINE. Not a bit of it! Don't be so hypocritical. In rehearsals you're all dying to make up your own lines, you know you are. Go on. Take the plunge. You know your characters ... You know the plot ... God dammit, what else is there to the theatre but that? A situation and some characters and then some talk – that's all! And after an hour or so you have an interval and they sell ice-creams and chocolates. All the rest is literary stuff and you know it!

ACTOR LAPINET (*shocked*). Oh but come, my dear maestro, certain works do carry a message!

ANTOINE. All right then, if you've got one, here's your chance, let's have it. We'll have a touch of the avant-garde. Off you go. I'm dead. I can't say another word. (*He adds kindly.*) You may object that it's slightly against union rules, but as I'm asking you to work at something more difficult, I'll double your salaries, how's that?

ACTOR LAPINET (*grandly, nevertheless a little beady-eyed*). Oh, I wasn't referring to that aspect of the matter, dear maestro ...

The characters look at each other, nonplussed. They watch him as he lies there, eyes shut, and then gradually, as they sink into the mood of it, their faces all take on a look of sadness. But still no one has yet spoken.

ANTOINE (*eyes closed, hands joined together*). Of course, if you wait too long the scene will fall flat on the floor.

ACTOR MARCELLIN (*taking the plunge at last*). To think he's lying there.

ACTOR LAPINET. In that little box.

ACTOR MARCELLIN. And him so active and full of life always.

ACTOR CRAVATAR (*with a poor attempt at conviction*). It's hardest for those that are left.

ANTOINE (*eyes closed, hands together*). That's very good. Very modern. Go on.

The cast look at each other, anguished. They have visibly come to a dead end. The ACTOR MARCELLIN *eventually flings out his arms and blurts out.*

ACTOR MARCELLIN. Words fail us!

ANTOINE (*irritably, between clenched teeth*). Don't admit it! You can be modern, but not to that extent.

ACTOR LAPINET (*with a sudden flash of historical inspiration*). Nothing in his life became him like the leaving of it.

ANTOINE. That was Charles I! Talk about me, damn you!

ACTOR CRAVATAR (*a brainwave at last*). It's an irreparable loss to the theatre!

ANTOINE. There. You've hit the right note! Press on.

ACTOR LAPINET. It's always the best who go first . . .

ACTOR CRAVATAR. Do you think he suffered much?

ACTOR MARCELLIN. They say not.

ACTOR LAPINET. I just can't take it in. I had lunch with him only last week – little did we think . . . We had some superb oysters . . .

ACTOR MARCELLIN. Little did any of us think . . . Him least of all.

ACTOR CRAVATAR. How old was he, exactly?

ACTOR MARCELLIN. Fifty-three.

ACTOR CRAVATAR. Really? I thought he was older than that. I thought he was fifty-four.

ACTOR LAPINET (*bringing his hand up to his bald patch, a little anguished*). Fifty-three. He was terribly young!

ACTOR MARCELLIN. Yes, but he was always chesty, you know.

A short pause, while they hunt for words, then CRAVATAR, *for want of anything new to say, repeats, heartfeltedly.*

ACTOR CRAVATAR. It's an irreparable loss to the theatre.

ANTOINE. You said that once. (*He sits up, dispirited and looks at them.*) It's feeble. Very feeble. If I were really dead you wouldn't have thrown me any bouquets. And there are the women, just drooping about and sighing. Widows pouring with tears, but speechless ... It's a good thing I didn't try to write that scene, I can see that. You don't say very much before the living, before the dead you say nothing at all ... (*He takes* ESTELLE's *hand and looks at her strangely.*) Have I no chance at all of ever knowing what you were – widow of mine? Perhaps nobody very much, after all. We build a mystery out of people and half the time there isn't one. A young woman who was bored, no more to it than that. (*He asks suddenly.*) Did you ever love me, do you think?

ACTRESS ESTELLE (*troubled*). I don't know.

ANTOINE (*with a smile*). Of course you don't. As a girl though, you seemed so loving ...

ACTRESS ESTELLE. In the part she's so hard, always ...

ANTOINE (*quietly*). That was a defence, perhaps ... (*He adds, drolly.*) Besides, I wrote the part myself – which isn't quite fair either. (*He muses a little, makes an odd little gesture and sighs.*) We'll never know anything. One never does. One dies not knowing. (*He adds.*) But maybe there was nothing to know. (*He looks at them, smiling a little abstractedly and says suddenly.*) You know what? I think we'd better give up trying to do this play!

ACTOR LAPINET (*breathtaken*). What? But, you dragged us all this way!

ANTOINE. Very irresponsible of me to make you come so far . . .
and all of you looking your parts so well . . . No, I think it's best
if friendship and love remain as concepts without faces. (*He looks
at them with a kind of anguish and then suddenly gives a shout of
laughter, pointing to* CRAVATAR.) And to cap it all I made an
enormous error of casting! It was you, of course, who should
have played the critic! I'm mad! You're the character to the life! I
see you with a small moustache . . . It's hallucinating! Hallucinating! It's him! Him to the life! It's Cravatar!

> *He bursts into wild laughter, still pointing at the dazed* CRAVA-
> TAR. *He cries, like the phonograph.*

ANTOINE. Are you there, Cravatar? Are you there, Cravatar?
Are you there, Cravatar?

> *The actors looking at him, nonplussed. The lights go down.*
> ANTOINE's *laugh is heard during the blackout. When the lights
> come up again we are back in a winter's evening. All the charac-
> ters are there, their real selves again, grouped around the*
> LAWYER *who is draining a big tankard of beer.*

LAWYER (*finishing his story*). After that abortive theatrical venture, which was in fact his last extravaganza, Monsieur de St
Flour found himself alone for good. It was then he realized
apparently, how lightly, at the throw of a die, almost, he had let
that young woman go. (*He leans over to* ESTELLE *who is sitting
stiffly beside him.*) If you will allow me to be frank, Madame –
she alone, in the course of a lifetime of illusions and inconse-
quence, had brought him, belatedly, a kind of reality . . . But
accustomed as he was to inventing everything, out of anything
that came to hand – no doubt he only grew aware of it after the
event . . . For him, teller of so many tales, reality was a thing
he'd never been familiar with.

> *A pause. He carries straight on, with a smile, lost in his memories.*

I had got to know Monsieur de St Flour very well, from long
nights together chatting, over countless mugs of beer.

MARCELLIN (*exclaiming*). Had he taken to drinking beer?

LAWYER. Yes.

MARCELLIN (*glass in hand*). Wonders will never cease. He used to
loathe it. Your modest white wine, yes, at a pinch —

LAWYER (*with a smile*). He'd taken to it. Monsieur de St Flour had
sensed, in this close, harsh country – where human beings
talk baldly to each other, and never about what they really
feel – that only at the bottom of the fifth or sixth tankard
will you find, if you look for it, a little human feeling and self
release.

ESTELLE (*wryly*). And may one ask what essential thing it was he
found at the bottom of the last tankard on your nights of
intimacy?

LAWYER (*quietly*). There's nothing to be found here, Madame, at
the bottom of the last tankard. No more than with you in your
last glass of wine. The mirage of a kind of truth, perhaps, in a
flash of insight – truth which experience reveals as most
deceptive the next morning, when the drink wears off. You go
back to what you were, a courteous and distant French playwright and a dull old German lawyer. And in the end, you
realize that you've told each other nothing.

*He drains his big tankard, his thoughts elsewhere. There is a
pause. Then* ESTELLE *asks suddenly, in the silence, her voice
sounding different for the first time since the beginning of the
play.*

ESTELLE. Did he feel very lonely in the last months?

LAWYER. Yes, Madame.

ESTELLE. He had a wife and children six hundred miles away and
he was alone from choice. Did he know that?

LAWYER. Yes.

ESTELLE (*in a slightly husky voice, almost shyly*). Perhaps all he
needed was a signal . . .

LAWYER (*quietly*). Loneliness is a fearsome trap. Lay a finger on it and it snaps shut.

ESTELLE (*with a kind of resentful tenderness, murmurs*). Antoine ended his life like a sulky child . . .

LAWYER (*gently*). Perhaps. But do grown-ups – who have different problems on their minds, ever seriously ask themselves why a child should start to sulk?

Another pause.

CRAVATAR (*heavily*). Antoine died like a dog, agreed, but how many outstretched hands did he brush aside? How many chances of love did he squander? (*He says suddenly, strangely, after a pause.*) I loved him at eighteen – when we were both studying for our degrees. I admired him. I dreamed of him, at night, as I might have a girl. He did everything more effortlessly than anyone else, without even bothering to work, taking a chance on it all. He was Antoine de St Flour, whose mother's chauffeur used to pick me up after classes, with the young master . . . (*He stops and then cries out suddenly.*) I had to squeeze the last ounce out of my working lad's brain, between these two thick hands, like my stonemason father's, instead of writing what I fancied, for fun, like him, at a café table! I had to turn myself into a swotting bore and take everything seriously, like a yokel, to find something I could be sure of at last – since I'd been given nothing at the starting post. The world of the poor crumbles when they see the rich turn life into a joke. It's like a blow in the face. So then they become critics! And mark plays nought out of ten. Deservedly.

The dog has started howling again louder than ever. CRAVATAR *bounds over to the rifle rack, seizes a weapon and hunts around furiously for cartridges, yelling.*

Right! They'll have to put that dog down some time, if they sell the house. So somebody had better buckle to and do it!

ESTELLE (*with a cry, transformed, hurling herself on to him like a small rabid animal*). No! Not his dog! Don't you touch his dog! Don't you touch his guns! Stop saying all those things about him! I'm sick of listening to you and your hatred!

CRAVATAR (*murmuring, deflated*). Why, Estelle . . .

A pause.

ESTELLE (*dully*). I loved Antoine, once. And then it turned to hate. But I hate those who hate *him*.

CRAVATAR (*murmuring*). Do you still love him, Estelle?

ESTELLE (*crying out through her tears*). I don't know! I don't know! I don't know any more! You never did know where you were with him. And that goes on . . .

She sinks into her chair, weeping. VALÉRIE *sighs, distantly puffing at a long cigarette holder.*

VALÉRIE. Estelle my pet, when will you stop battling with yourself?

ESTELLE *has taken a grip on herself and checked her tears.* VALÉRIE *goes on nonchalantly.*

In Antoine's day – that's when you should have cried out like that, just once. He might have heard you.

A pause.

ESTELLE (*locked up in herself again, pitiably*). I couldn't. I've never known how. I wasn't bred to it.

VALÉRIE (*with a sort of smiling nostalgia*). Basically, Antoine's trouble was that he could only believe in what he imagined for himself . . .

A pause. Then MARCELLIN *adds, pouring oil as always, in the renewed silence.*

MARCELLIN. What a delightful man he was, though! What a fascinating storyteller! And such an agreeable friend to have. Everything was a joke to him. Lord, the laughs we had together, truly! I don't understand you. I never suffered from that inconsequential side. He used to tell everyone that I didn't know a thing about medicine – and he may well have been right, we're all of us in that boat. Half the time I thought his plays were execrable, and when I could be witty at his expense, across a dinner-table, I didn't think twice. It was all in fair fight, good Lord! (*He goes on, a little uneasily.*) He resented it when I left him in the lurch with acute appendicitis, yes – but I put him on to a first-rate surgeon and I did have a very tempting house-party to go to at Deauville. On the other hand, he never came to my mother's funeral, because he overslept until noon that day in some bawdy house. That's friendship! I don't understand you. You complicate the simplest things. I got on splendidly with Antoine. What about you, Lapinet? Say something . . .

They all turn to LAPINET. *He is asleep in his chair, gently snoring.*

He's gone to sleep. You see? – his conscience is perfectly clear too.

CARLOTTA (*trenchantly*). Right! Either way, Antoine is dead and all these questionings are idle chatter. (*She gets painfully to her feet.*) Now that's enough about Antoine. I'm dropping. I'd suggest we all went up to bed. It's done me good, that ointment of yours, my poppet. Antoine never gave any of us much. We didn't give him very much either. Turn over; fresh page. The books are balanced. The accounts are straight.

Everyone gets up to go out. GABRIELLE *has gone to waken* LAPINET.

GABRIELLE. Rabbitskin! Rabbitskin! Sleepybyes! It's up early in the morning! The Consul is coming to unveil the plaque on Antoine's house.

LAPINET (*waking, flustered*). Oh, sorry . . . I dropped off. Do you know, I was dreaming that Antoine had finally agreed to join the Academy of Letters and I was making the inaugural speech ...

GABRIELLE *helps him up. They are all on their way out. They burst out laughing and the curtain falls.*

Act Four

In front of the closed tabs, there suddenly bursts forth a rendering of the Marseillaise, played so very much too fast that it sounds vaguely comical. The curtain rises towards the end of the Anthem on the sunlit set. It is morning. ALEXANDER *and* ANÉMONE, *arms round each other's waists, are standing at the window, looking out. Closing bars of the Marseillaise.*

ALEXANDER (*wryly*). A bit fast. I suppose they meant it to sound Parisian.

ANÉMONE (*distressed*). It's ridiculous! All of it!

ALEXANDER. No, it isn't! I'm sure Father would have got a lot of fun out of it! Look! They're unfurling the French flag. The ultimate in Germanic graciousness. They must have made it overnight out of little girls' petticoats. It's all wavy. Carlotta is standing to attention, her veils blowing in the wind. There's Cravatar, sunk in grief, with his face a solid mask. Marcellin very grave. Lapinet oozing like a tap. Splendid performances, one and all.

ANÉMONE. And the dog?

ALEXANDER. They sent it down to the farm so it wouldn't disturb the ceremony. Each time it saw Cravatar it went for him. But the best thing is the plaque. How they must have scurried to get it ready while the guests were here. A marble slab, made of wood and hand painted. It looks like an inn sign.

ANÉMONE. It's horrible.

ALEXANDER. No, it isn't, it's very funny! Papa is doubled up with laughter at this very moment.

ANÉMONE (*asking suddenly*). What are all those children doing?

ALEXANDER. Don't worry, they aren't his. That's the choir.

ANÉMONE. Are they going to sing?

ALEXANDER. I'm afraid they are.

ANÉMONE (*trying to pull him out*). We've got to go down. We ought to be there.

ALEXANDER (*kindly*). Yes, but we'll be with the others and there aren't so many chances of being alone together. We can pay tribute to Father's memory from up here.

He has taken her tenderly in his arms, smiling. She sighs, but puts up no resistance.

ANÉMONE. Go on! Laugh, do! But when a girl has loved a man as exceptional as that, you must see that she can't ever again let . . . That's why I'm sending all the money he left me to Doctor Schweizer! That's why I want to go to Africa to nurse lepers – hideous lepers – all the rest of my life.

ALEXANDER (*softly*). That wouldn't give him any pleasure at all, my heart, not if I know him – as I'm beginning to. He loathed the poor and wretched of this earth. He said they were rapacious creditors.

ANÉMONE (*still in his arms, cries out again*). That's why I don't ever want to be in a young man's arms again! That's why I never go dancing now, why I never go out, why I don't want anything to give me any pleasure again, ever! That's why I can't wait to be old! (*She asks.*) Will it take long, do you think?

ALEXANDER (*gently, holding her*). Very long.

ANÉMONE (*whimpering suddenly, both touching and funny*). Oh, it's so exhausting being young!

ALEXANDER (*gently, quite unmocking*). It's frightful, my heart. And it's frightful being dead too. Two different things – and nothing you can do about either.

ANÉMONE (*wide-eyed, still moaning*). I don't ever want to forget him! Ever!

ALEXANDER. No, my heart.

They look at each other for an instant, both a little anguished. Then, at last, they kiss. ANÉMONE *brings her hands slowly up to* ALEXANDER's *as if to free herself, then suddenly she stops half-way, touched and rueful at the same time.*

ANÉMONE. Oh, your hands are exactly the same as his! It's terrible . . .

He kisses her again, and this time ANÉMONE'S *arms cross round his neck.*

ALEXANDER (*breaking away slightly, says kindly*). Poor Father. (*He shakes himself and cries.*) What beasts we are. We've deserted him. Let's look and see what they're doing to him. We can't let him go through all that alone. We've got to raise the man's morale!

He draws her to the window. Outside, the silence which precedes the crucial moment of the ceremony. ALEXANDER *says comically.*

The solemn moment. The Consul's pulling his little box out of his pocket. He's clearing his throat. (*He shouts suddenly through the window.*) Hold on, Father! We're here!

ANÉMONE (*pulling him back, helpless with laughter*). You're mad! Be quiet! They turned round!

The CONSUL'S *voice, absurd, emphatic, rises in the silence.*

CONSUL (*off*). In the name of the President of the French Republic, and by virtue of the powers invested in me, I award you, Antoine de St Flour, the posthumous title of Knight Companion of the Legion of Honour!

ALEXANDER (*comically*). That's it! They got him! Cravatar's livid, he's only got the oak leaves.

The German Anthem bursts forth suddenly, with fanfare. ALEXANDER *roars with laughter.*

The final insult! The girl friend's anthem! Concerted leap to attention on the German side. Our lot are a bit embarrassed. The *Marseillaise* is one thing. But the *Uber Alles*! Carlotta's looking daggers. Doing a thing like that to *her*, after robbing her of Alsace and Lorraine!

They both start laughing like maniacs and dancing a sort of comic minuet to the rhythm of the German Anthem. ALEXANDER *goes back to the window.*

Look! Supreme Teutonic ruse! The pastor has pulled a sheet of paper from his pocket. *He's* going to deliver his speech too. They've seen it. Stampede! They'll miss the Munich train! Cravatar whispers to Lapinet, who whispers to Marcellin, who whispers to the Lawyer, who whispers to the Burgomaster. They've sent a delegation. Done! They've dissuaded the pastor, he's folding up his speech, looking very thwarted. Saved! We'll catch the train!

The German Anthem has just finished, there is the sound of a crowd shuffling outside. ALEXANDER, *at the window like a radio commentator, declaims.*

No! Reversal! The schoolmaster's not standing for that, the old Prussian! He's marshalling his choir! Surge of panic among the French troops. Desperation! Mutiny! But nothing can halt the Pomeranian Grenadiers! Charge! They've captured the terrain! Breakthrough! Might is right! It's total rout! It's Sedan!

The choir breaks out in high piercing tones to an unexpectedly brisk rhythm. ALEXANDER *concludes.*

They've drained the bitter cup down to the dregs. Now see if Europe isn't plunged into a holocaust after this!

This whole scene has been punctuated by helpless giggles from ANÉMONE *and* ALEXANDER, *as they stand in each others arms. When the choir breaks out, they start to dance a sort of Bavarian polka, which gradually merges into a tender embrace.* FRIDA *and the little* MANSERVANT *enter, loaded down with suitcases. They make several rapid trips to the gay rhythm of the choir. At the end of the scene, the stage will be littered with everybody's luggage. Directly the last bars die out, everyone will come charging in, and the rest of the scene will be played at frantic speed. People dash upstairs, dash down again, look for their luggage. There is one continuous rush.* CARLOTTA *has come in first, hobbling painfully but swiftly on her stick.*

CARLOTTA. The hogs! Forty-five solid minutes on our feet listening to their ditties! Now we're going to have to run. Ha! – when they start their music-making, that lot —! If we hadn't put our foot down we'd have had the whole of Lohengrin!

MARCELLIN. Quick! Quick! Let's get out! They're quite likely to corner us for a toast in their best hock. At least we headed off the pastor!

CARLOTTA. A pastor for Antoine! How he'd have loathed that!

MARCELLIN. He was a Catholic, wasn't he?

CARLOTTA. Isn't everybody? In unimportant things Antoine always took the line of least resistance.

LAPINET. How are we going to manage for transport, with that one motor?

MARCELLIN. The Consul has a gigantic limousine, it will take at least five. There won't be time for more than one trip.

CARLOTTA. Let's go together, my duck. You can tell me your story of the little girl who swallowed the soap. Come on, let's cheer up! I loathe funerals – they give you black thoughts . . . We must have a very jolly journey!

They go out.

CRAVATAR (*going to* ESTELLE *and taking her suitcase*). Shall we ride together?

ESTELLE. If you like.

CRAVATAR. Can we meet when we get back to Paris, Estelle? It's been too long since we saw each other.

ESTELLE (*smiling, after a slight hesitation*). If you want to.

CRAVATAR. You've no idea, for a bachelor critic, how boring all those first nights are. Will you come to the theatre with me sometimes, when your time of mourning's over?

ESTELLE (*with another smile*). We'll see . . . a little later on . . .

CRAVATAR. I'm sure you'll find the new playwrights very interesting. There's an amazing movement just beginning to take
shape. An irresistible gust of new air, sweeping all the old claptrap away.

*He has gone out busily with the luggage, threading his way
through the others as they scurry about.*

GABRIELLE (*face to face with* LAPINET, *moved*). So there it is,
Rabbitskin.

LAPINET (*moist-eyed*). There it is, Gabrielle – What are you
going to do when you get back to Paris?

GABRIELLE. My housework! Five days of dust ...

LAPINET. Will you ask me to dinner sometimes?

GABRIELLE. If you don't mind my five flights of stairs ...

LAPINET. I'll find my young man's legs again. And I'll bring you
a bunch of flowers, like in the old days.

GABRIELLE. Then I'll do you my duck pasty. It's my triumph!
And then a nice sweet leg of lamb and to finish my apricot cream
with brandy.

LAPINET. And I'll bring some champagne!

GABRIELLE (*gaily*). We'll fill ourselves up to here! My husband
used to say, when you get old, all you've got left is the belly.

LAPINET (*gaily too*). And that will give us a chance to talk about
Antoine! No, no, let me take your bag.

GABRIELLE (*going out gaily*). It's a glorious day! I'm sure we're
going to have a most enjoyable journey ...

They go out.

VALÉRIE (*on her way out too*). Which motor are you going in,
Estelle? If we lose each other at Munich station, give me a call
as soon as you get home. We could meet at Patou's. I'm up to
my eyes! With this appointment of my husband's to Washington, I'm never away from the dressmakers'. Are you coming,
Anémone?

She goes swiftly out.

ALEXANDER. Are you going to Washington, too?

ANÉMONE. No. I've one more year of studying in Paris. I shall live with my great aunt. She's deaf as a newt and half blind.

ALEXANDER (*gaily*). Marvellous! May I come and see you?

ANÉMONE. As often as you like! All you have to do is keep quite still when she crosses the room. She can't tell a man from an aspidistra.

They both burst out laughing.

ALEXANDER. Oh, isn't living fun! Don't you think we're really too lucky?

ANÉMONE (*going out*). Too lucky, why?

ALEXANDER (*kindly as he goes out*). Coming to the same funeral!

ESTELLE is left standing motionless in the middle of the room, alone with the LAWYER. Outside, they are starting to close the shutters. The scene will finish in the half-dark.

ESTELLE. Are they shutting up the house?

LAWYER. That was Monsieur de St Flour's wish, after the cere-mony. To shut everything up. To leave the dust to settle over everything – to let the weeds grow in the garden. Frida is leav-ing too. She is going back home, to the village —

The room is quite dark now. Dull knocking is heard outside. The LAWYER explains.

Some of the shutters don't close properly. They're boarding them up.

ESTELLE is motionless, as if slightly engulfed. The LAWYER says gently, after a moment's respect for her silence.

We'll have to go or they'll shut us in . . .

A few more knocks farther off. The LAWYER muses a little. Then he says suddenly.

There's a very fine play by Chekhov, that Monsieur de St

Flour admired very much – he used to say it had haunted
him ever since he was twenty . . . And that ends this way too.
They sell an old family estate where people were once happy
and which nobody will ever come back to again. They board up
the shutters. And inside, they forget an old manservant who was
the spirit of the place and who will very likely die there. (*He
gives a sad little smile.*) I hope *we* won't forget anybody here.

A few more knockings on the shutters, afar off. The LAWYER
concludes, smiling.

Monsieur de St Flour admired that ending very much and he
used to say, in that funny way he had – 'It's too silly! To think
that wretch thought of it first! I'll never be able to use it myself,
they'd notice. Unless, of course, I served it up again with some
sort of twist to it . . .'

ESTELLE (*her thoughts elsewhere, as she goes out*). What was the
play?

LAWYER. *The Cherry Orchard.*

ESTELLE (*going out*). Don't know it. Antoine never mentioned it to
me. Or maybe I've forgotten . . .

They have gone out. The room is deserted and dark.
Abruptly, one last shaft of light goes out. The last shutter has
been closed. There are more hammerings, faintly heard. Then the
motor cars starting up and setting off. Then silence. Suddenly,
from some way away, recorded in the same light tempo in which
they were originally played, one hears the lines of the preceding
scene, spoken by faintly ghost-like voices.

MARCELLIN's VOICE. Quick! Quick! Let's get out! At least we
headed off the pastor!

CARLOTTA's VOICE. A pastor for Antoine! How he'd have loathed
that!

MARCELLIN'S VOICE. He was a Catholic, wasn't he?

CARLOTTA'S VOICE. Isn't everybody? In unimportant things
Antoine always took the line of least resistance.

CRAVATOR'S VOICE. I'm sure you'll find the new playwrights very interesting. There's an amazing movement beginning to take shape! An irresistible gust of fresh air sweeping all the old claptrap away.

GABRIELLE'S VOICE. I'll do you my duck pasty! It's my triumph. And then a nice sweet leg of lamb and to finish, my apricot cream with brandy.

LAPINET'S VOICE. Then I'll bring some champagne! And that will give us a chance to talk about Antoine!

ALEXANDER'S VOICE. Oh, isn't living fun! Don't you think we're lucky?

ANÉMONE'S VOICE. Lucky, why?

ALEXANDER'S VOICE. Coming to the same funeral!

ESTELLE'S VOICE. And what was the play?

LAWYER'S VOICE. *The Cherry Orchard.*

ESTELLE'S VOICE. Don't know it. Antoine never mentioned it to me. Or maybe I've forgotten.

> *There is a moment of silence, as prolonged as possible, in the empty set, and then the curtain falls.*

Methuen's Modern Plays

EDITED BY JOHN CULLEN

Shelagh Delaney	*A Taste of Honey*
	The Lion in Love
Max Frisch	*The Fire Raisers*
	Andorra
Jean Giraudoux	*Tiger at the Gates*
Simon Gray	*Spoiled*
Peter Handke	*Offending the Audience* and *Self-Accusation*
Rolf Hochhuth	*The Representative*
Heinar Kipphardt	*In the Matter of J. Robert Oppenheimer*
Arthur Kopit	*Chamber Music and other plays*
	Indians
Jakov Lind	*The Silver Foxes are Dead and other plays*
David Mercer	*On the Eve of Publication and other plays*
	After Haggerty
	Flint
John Mortimer	*The Judge*
	Five Plays
	Come as You Are
Joe Orton	*Crimes of Passion*
	Loot
	What the Butler Saw
	Funeral Games and *The Good and Faithful Servant*
Harold Pinter	*The Birthday Party*
	The Room and *The Dumb Waiter*
	The Caretaker
	A Slight Ache and other plays
	The Collection and *The Lover*
	The Homecoming
	Tea Party and other plays
	Landscape and *Silence*
	Old Times
David Selbourne	*The Damned*
Jean-Paul Sartre	*Crime Passionnel*
Boris Vian	*The Empire Builders*
Theatre Workshop and Charles Chilton	*Oh What a Lovely War*
Charles Wood	*'H'*

*   *   *

Methuen's Theatre Classics

*   *   *

Methuen's Playscripts